Living an
Extraordinary
Life

About This Book

Based on intensive work with over 500,000 people worldwide, this book demonstrates that we all have everything it takes to live an extraordinary life —if we are willing to take charge of our lives and discover the true meaning of personal responsibility.

Like diets we don't follow, "self-help" books have become cliché-ridden shopping lists for what doesn't work. They are as likely to generate a "Doonesbury" spoof as improvements in people's lives. Often the only thing they improve is the thickness of their authors' wallets.

Prescribing solutions is almost always ineffective and self-defeating. Until you are good and ready, you are not going to follow even the most well-meaning advice.

But if you are truly ready for growth and change, and if your facilitator is gifted, it is possible. The key is insightful coaching and a lot of penetrating questions, heart-to-heart questions that reach deep inside and ask you to address issues you can no longer afford to avoid.

In this, Robert White's first book, he says, "I don't have the answers for your life, but I know for certain that you do. There are no rules in these pages, nothing conceptual or theoretical to be mastered or to memorize. It is simply an inquiry into what is possible for each of us in the areas of life we truly care about most: our relationships, career, personal identity, joy in living and connection to spirit."

LIVING AN EXTRAORDINARY LIFE

Unlocking Your Potential
for Success, Joy and Fulfillment

BY **ROBERT WHITE**

Copyright 2006 by Robert White

All rights reserved. No part of this book may be reproduced in any form or by any electronic or mechanical means, including information storage and retrieval systems, without permission in writing from the publisher, except by a reviewer who may quote brief passages in a review.

Published by Extraordinary Resources llc
Extraordinary Resources
5200 South Ulster St., Suite 1109
Greenwood Village, CO 80111
USA
(303) 993-4640

Edited and with contributions by Peter Sherwood. Additional contributions by Keith Bentz and Mitch Feigenberg

Additional editorial services: Debra Alford and Norma Gairdner

Marketing Consultant: Robert Middleton
Design and production: Canright & Paule, Inc., Chicago

ISBN-13: 978-0-9753585-0-4
ISBN-10: 0-9753585-0-2

Dedicated with love
to the memory of Art Marshall.
Art was a friend, colleague and
a powerful example of the
possibility that lives in everyone
for making a difference; for
creating a world that works for all:
one world, one people.

Thank You...

Hubert Humphrey once said, "I learned more about economics from one South Dakota dust storm than I did in all my years in college." So it is with my own education, and while it lacks a great deal, it has never been short on quality teachers. From these insightful and innovative people I have learned so much, both directly and by osmosis. Some lessons came to me from a simple phrase caught, then fumbled, and caught again much later as I grew to understand the deeper truth of what had been said; while other messages reached me unspoken, from the privilege of being in the company of those whose instruction came by example alone.

Until I began this book, I imagined my role as author and teacher. I could hardly have been more wrong. It quickly became a learning experience and a journey for which I will be forever grateful.

I can't acknowledge everyone who has contributed to my education (and consequently to this book), or to even begin to thank them adequately. Their contributions have taken many forms, from formal classroom or a walk along a river, to their writings and speeches, or through their examples of how to live conscious, extraordinary lives. I have directly thanked some of these wonderful people. Others will learn here of my appreciation for the gift they are in my life.

There are no words adequate to express my gratitude and love to my mother Margaret White, brothers Hank, Sam and Jimmy and sisters Marian and Patricia; former wives and teachers, Geraldine, Kathrine and Dianna; the family that taught me about love—Joe, Helen, Michael and the entire Shalhoub clan; my birth children—Thomas, Gary, Gregory, Rob, Megan and Alicia; and my children-of-the-heart-and-spirit—Levi and Emily.

Every day for the past thirty years I've had the honor and privilege of working with my associates in Lifespring, ARC International, Balance Point International and Extraordinary Resources. I acknowledge that I've taught them a bit. This is a good place to acknowledge all that they've taught me. The members of this diverse, creative and committed group are models of love in action, living our vision and values daily and creating the environment of excellence and caring which supports me in all that I do. While the list of past and present associates is too long to print, my gratitude is total and personally directed to each of them.

While I must share credit for anything remotely brilliant with the people listed below, the errors and omissions are mine alone. Great teachers, heroes and friends include Mark Albion, Dr. A. T. Ariyaratne, John Babbs, Doug Belscher, Ken Blanchard, David Bork, Hyler Bracey, Landon Carter, Chin-Ning Chu, Dale Collins, Tom Crum, Robbie Delgado, Joe Dunkle, Werner Erhard, Alexander Everett, Stewart Esposito, Lara Ewing, Kenny Fischer, Robert Gass, Paul Harris, Hossca Harrison (and Jonah), Kate Hastings, Preston Hofer, Rick Huttner, Walt and Georgia Imhoff, Raz Ingrasci, Doak Jacoway, Jerry Jampolsky and Diane Cirincione, Joe Janiczek, Bill Johnson, Jim Jonell, Mat Juechter, Charlie Kiefer, Henri Landwirth, Martin Leaf, Tom and Flame Lutes, Isamu Masuda, Tom McCloskey, Patricia McLagan, Mat Molitch, Harrison Owen, Jagdish Parikh, Larry Proffit, Michael Ray, John Renesch, Herb Ross, Alby Segall, David Sibbet, Mo Siegel, Eric Smulders, Dorothy and Hal Thau, Michael and Justine Toms, Steve Vannoy, Toshizo "Tom" Watanabe, Victoria and Ian Watson, Gunther Weil, Dick Whiteley, and Judith and Bob Wright.

Included in my "most valued teachers" list with love and gratitude and sadly no longer with us physically are John Denver, John Enright, John Jones, Kim McMillan, Koichi Shimazu and Paul Sung.

To express my gratitude to these friends and mentors, I could do no better than to quote John Denver from the song he composed and sang to celebrate his experience of our VisionQuest seminar:

> *The gift you are, like the very first breath of Spring*
> *The gift you are, all the joy that love can bring*
> *The gift you are, all of my dreams come true*
> *The gift you are, the gift of you*

With love and respect,

Robert White

MY TEN CENTS' WORTH:
A PERSONAL NOTE

By Peter Sherwood

One of funny man Bill Cosby's first recordings was a hilarious reflection on his college days as a physical education major. It was called, "Why is There Air?" He describes the philosophy students wandering around campus asking profound metaphysical questions like, "What is the universe?" and "Why is there air?' "Hell," said Cosby, "any phys-ed student knows why there's air. There's air to blow up basketballs, blow up volleyballs. God, and they call us dumb, for cryin' out loud?!"

I could relate to that. I used to have a black belt in asking questions that led nowhere. Then, in 1992, I found myself in a situation in which I was asked different kinds of questions—questions that led somewhere. They were tough questions, questions that demanded I look much deeper into my life than I'd ever wanted to. The situation was a seminar presented by Robert White's company at that time.

Robert White has been at the sharp end of personal effectiveness training for 30 years. He was—and is—committed to making a difference for people. More precisely, making a difference for normal, relatively successful people like you and me. Together, he and I are responsible for saving my life, no small matter when you consider the positive repercussions for the Hong Kong income tax authorities and bar owners.

Robert's work is designed for emotionally and mentally healthy people who want to create extraordinary lives. It is rooted in efforts begun after the Second World War to create powerful learning technologies that strengthen our abilities to live full, complete lives and accomplish the goals we set for ourselves. My start in the seminar was a bit different. Although I was enjoying a successful career, I had just returned from a trip to Russia to be suddenly and unceremoniously whacked by massive depression. It left me barely able to function. I looked like I'd spent ten years in a Soviet Gulag. Emerging slowly from the darkness with the help of a good doctor, I knew deep down that the real battle was still to come.

I was lucky. A friend took me to lunch and described some of the experiences in the seminar he'd just completed. He said, "Peter, I really want you to do this course. Tomorrow night there's an introductory event. I'd like you to come with me as my guest. How about it?" I said I would go, and I did, even though I was very skeptical about the whole thing—especially about how I might turn my life around through some seminar. After that guest event I signed up for the next course, pretty much on the basis that my life was not working and I needed to do something about it. I felt that if I didn't find some answers, and soon, I might well return to the hell of depression.

The seminars were not an easy journey, but with a lot of demanding work I was able to discover what was driving my moods and behaviors. I was able to break out and begin the challenging and rewarding process of reinventing myself.

A few years after I completed this powerful work, my 18-year-old son did the seminar programs. Within six months his school grades went from failing nearly every subject to getting B's and C's—progress not much short of astounding. His school took all the credit. I know different. Today, he is a successful college student and a star on the swim team.

Robert White is an outstanding example of what one very determined man can achieve when he has passion and a clear vision. He embodies everything the American president, Calvin Coolidge, said about determination:

"Nothing in the world can take the place of persistence. Talent will not; nothing is more common than unsuccessful men with talent. Genius will not; unrewarded genius is almost a proverb. Education will not; the world is full of educated derelicts. Persistence and determination alone are omnipotent."

Robert stared penury in the eye for many years before his personal effectiveness and corporate executive training programs gained their deserved worldwide success. If not for his dogged persistence, hanging on to his dream when he should have known better, the work would never have made it to Hong Kong. I do not allow myself to think what my life might have become without it.

While this book can only partially replicate the power of the seminar experience, it excites me because, like the seminars, it does not attempt to tell people how to live their lives. No rules, no dogma, no cosmic mumbo-jumbo; just an approach to living successfully that seems to work.

Peter Sherwood is an Australian author, journalist, newspaper columnist and public relations professional based in Hong Kong.

ORDINARY OR **EXTRAORDINARY**

Why do some people lead extraordinary lives and others don't?

Living an extraordinary life doesn't happen by chance or luck. Observation of our seminar and coaching participants, plus numerous other studies undertaken over the past two decades, convincingly demonstrates that otherwise ordinary men and women who create extraordinary results—regardless of age, nationality or education—exhibit many of the same behaviors, language patterns and ways of being. In other words, there are things that you can do and ways to speak and ways to be that will definitely support you in creating the results you want—in your career, your relationships, your finances, your health—in every area of your life.

The building blocks we've discovered that are essential to living an extraordinary life are **Awareness, Responsibility** and **Communication**. This conceptual framework is the foundation of our work at ARC Worldwide. If you want real success in life, if you want to live an extraordinary life, I recommend you learn more and apply those lessons in action. That's the purpose of this book.

Contents

My Ten Cents' Worth: A Personal Note... i
Ordinary or Extraordinary?... iii

Part 1: How It All Began, and What It's All About
    1 The Power of One... 2
    2 Awareness, Responsibility and Communication............................ 5
    3 You Always Make the Best Choice.. 11

Part 2: Awareness
    4 Don't Believe Anything I Say... 21
    5 The Meaning of Life... 25
    6 A Small Matter of Miracles... 29
    7 The Laws of Scarcity and Abundance....................................... 34
    8 Insanity is Not Just for the Insane... 36
    9 Intention and the Titanic.. 44
    10 Your Uncomfortable Comfort Zone... 52
    11 The Most Common Self-Limiting Belief in the World:
        "I Am Not Enough".. 61
    12 Changing Gears: Life's Better When You First
        Switch Into Neutral... 70
    13 Attitude's No Platitude.. 74

Part 3: Responsibility
    14 To Choose or Not to Choose?... 80
    15 Do You Really Have to?.. 82
    16 Feel Great or Grungy–There is No Third Way........................... 87
    17 Sitting on the Fence is a Choice, Too....................................... 91
    18 Responsibility: Do You Feel Like a Snowflake in an Avalanche?....... 97
    19 Being Right is a Life-Threatening Condition............................. 111
    20 Who is That Fabulous Person Hiding Under Your Image?............ 118
    21 Time to Wake Up! You've Got the Wrong Goal......................... 122
    22 Wishful Thinking Versus Reality.. 127

23 There is No Hope... 130
24 Redefining Success.. 132
25 Learning to Love Your Mistakes... 136
26 Embracing Change: The Truly Difficult Hug........................... 141
27 Everybody Wants to Go to Heaven, but Nobody Wants to Die........ 143
28 You're Living Life Back to Front... 147
29 So, You Want to be Happy... 153
30 More Bucks or Yen or Euros Will Make it Better, Right?................156
31 The Greatest Love of All... 165
32 What You Resist, Persists.. 169

Part 4: Communication
33 A Soaring Eagle, or a Jabbering Parrot?.................................. 178
34 Be Selfish: Give, Give, Give–Then Give Some More..................... 192
35 What If?... 200
36 And Now (Finally): How Can you Become a New Person?............ 204

Let Us Hear From You..210
Additional Copies... 210
Speaking Engagements..210
The Achieving Extraordinary Success Home Study Program 211
Executive Coaching, Team Leadership Development
    and Organizational Culture Change Programs..................................211
Reference Acknowledgements 212
About the Author 214

~ Part 1 ~

How It All Began, and
What It's All About

~ 1 ~

THE POWER OF ONE

*All my life I wanted to be somebody.
I should have been more specific.*

Woody Allen

When a customer asked the bookstore clerk for directions to the Self-Help section, he was a bit surprised at the answer he received: "To tell you would be self-defeating." And so it is with this book.

When it comes to having a more productive and fulfilling life, there are no easy answers. This book is simply a guide to what is possible, based on the work we have done in public and corporate seminars with hundreds of thousands of people. There is no list of ideal habits, or a "ten steps to success" program here. Only you and you alone can create the kind of life you want to have.

So let's be clear. This book alone cannot:
- make you happier
- raise your self-confidence or self-esteem
- cause you to be more positive about life
- make your life more purposeful, productive or exciting
- help your relationships work better
- make you more effective

It can't. Only you can change your life.

This is only a book, a bunch of words on a printed page. If it could change your life, that would make it—and me—responsible for your success and well being, with no control over your own life. Thank goodness, changing your life is your job. Even if I could do it, I don't wish to be responsible for your life or anyone else's; it's a full-time job handling my own life.

And this is how it should be. There is no way to find personal power without taking control of your own life. In fact, that's what true personal power is: being in charge of your own life. We call this responsibility, the ability to respond to one's own life situations. To imagine that another human being, even one with some useful ideas, can somehow take responsibility for your life, is to stumble around begging for trouble. It leaves you like Nasrudin, the character in the Sufi Tales who lost his keys in front of the door to his house, but was looking for them out under a street lamp. When someone asked him why, he said "Because there's more light out here."

Looking to someone else for the answers is like that. It may seem easier and less work, but you're looking in the wrong place. To find the answers for your own life, you need to look where the answers are: within yourself.

So as this book's author, independent of your active involvement, I am absolutely unable to make your life better. However, I do know how you can. The first step is to begin looking in a completely new way at your life; to consider the full range of possibilities that being human represents; in short, to begin to entertain the possibility that the life of an ordinary person—you—could be extraordinary.

Daniel Goleman, in his wonderful book *Emotional Intelligence*, says:

> "What factors are at play… when people of a high IQ flounder, and those of modest IQ do surprisingly well? the difference quite often lies in the abilities called here emotional intelligence, which include self-control, zeal and persistence, and the ability to motivate oneself. I can foresee a day when education will routinely include inculcating essential human competencies such as self-awareness, self-control and empathy, and the arts of listening, resolving conflicts, and cooperation."

Chance or luck may play a part in living an extraordinary life. Yet waiting around to "get lucky" is analogous to your chances of winning the lottery. My research, my personal life experience and the privilege of working with over 500,000 clients during the past twenty years, demonstrate that ordinary men and women who create outstanding results—regardless of age, nationality or education—exhibit remarkably similar language patterns, behaviors and ways of being. In other words, knowing how to live an extraordinary life is not a mystery. There are established, proven things you can speak, do and ways to be that will effectively support you in creating he results you want, in your career, your relationships, your finances, your health, your spiritual growth—in every area of your life.

The purpose of this book is to share what I've learned about this most important subject—how you can live an extraordinary life. It is organized around what we have learned to be essential "building blocks," some ideas, principles and methods that will assist you in doing the real work of creating a brighter future for your self.

Remember, getting what you want in life is simple; however, it is often not easy.

When people ask me about the work I do, sometimes there is an opening to get beyond the simple, trite expressions like "experiential education for adults and organizations that want better results." When that opportunity exists, my simplified answer is to say, "We assist people and organizations in becoming aware, understanding and learning from their past experiences so that they leave those experiences where they belong—in their past. Then we assist people and organizations to get responsible, to "tell the truth" about their current reality, free of any "spin," guilt or discomfort, so that they can recognize their strengths and areas that need attention. Finally, we assist people and organizations in creating new communication abilities based on consciously choosing a new future. We give them useful tools for reaching their goals, contributing to others and for living an extraordinary life."

That's also the purpose of this book and you'll notice woven throughout is a framework for you to follow if you truly want to leave your past behind (Awareness), to accurately describe your current reality (Responsibility) and to choose a great future (Communication)—in short, this book is about how to create an extraordinary life.

The book's framework is **Awareness, Responsibility** and **Communication**. These concepts are at the heart of the work we've done with hundreds of thousands of people. These ideas have changed those people's lives for the better and they can do the same for you—assuming you are willing to do the work of bringing greater awareness, responsibility and communication to your life.

~ 2 ~

AWARENESS, RESPONSIBILITY AND COMMUNICATION

The essence of living an extraordinary life
Simple, and not necessarily easy.

A few years ago a television commercial became part of popular culture in the United States. Victor Kiam of Remington exclaimed that he "liked the shaver so much, I bought the company." My version of that commercial would be "I liked the concepts of Awareness, Responsibility and Communication so much I named one of my companies ARC."

Over twenty years ago I was working with the brilliant and innovative psychologist, researcher, training designer and professor, Dr. John Enright. The late Dr. Enright played a seminal role in the design of our experiential seminars that have graduated over 500,000 people. He also did extensive work developing the abilities of our seminar leaders and he named one of those programs ARC: an acronym for Awareness, Responsibility and Communication.

It was John's observation that these three qualities were indispensable building blocks for successful living and I agreed. He graciously agreed to allow me to use ARC as our corporate name and it served us well – a constant reminder of our mission to bring those qualities to people and organizations.

Awareness, Responsibility and Communication…these are the ABCs of creating an extraordinary life. Like learning the ABCs as a child, learning the "ARCs" is simple and fundamental, though not necessarily easy.

Mastering ARC is a process much like learning the alphabet. It requires a similar step-by-step approach, laying a solid foundation, and then continually building on that foundation to achieve more and more understanding and insight. If we are willing to go through the process of learning to put higher levels of Awareness, Responsibility and Communication into practice in our lives, we can gain much more than just an intellectual understanding. Like a child who masters the ABCs, and in so doing lays the foundation for a life of literacy and learning, we can use the tools of Awareness, Responsibility and Communication to create new possibilities and an extraordinary future for ourselves, our families, our organizations and communities.

Awareness is the necessary beginning of any positive process of personal or organizational growth. People tend to succeed to the extent that they are aware of their essential purpose for existence, aware of a compelling vision for their lives, aware of and living consistent with a set of positive values and aware of short term goals that will take them to the next step of their development. If they aren't able to see things clearly, they will inevitably make mistakes based on false assumptions about themselves and others. This principle applies as much to any individual as to a major corporation, a society, or humanity at large.

Gaining deeper awareness is often compared to waking up, because when I am unaware, I am really asleep to what is going on around and even within me. Unfortunately, the kind of waking up that really opens new life possibilities is often forced upon us by dramatic, even traumatic, moments of crisis such as a painful ending to a relationship, a health emergency, business or financial failure, or a death in our family.

I'm a personal example of "waking up" as a result of a dramatic event and have often said that my first real awareness training was not the Mind Dynamics seminar I attended in 1969. It was a divorce from my first wife. These kinds of events can precipitate a "waking up" process that, when honestly confronted, can be the beginning of fresh insights and valuable life lessons.

To create an extraordinary life, I need the information that only a deep sense of self-awareness and awareness of others can provide. I need to be willing to honestly face my life and what is occurring within it. With awareness I get to see my underlying attitudes, habits and beliefs, and the behaviors that flow out of these foundational inner qualities. I get to see whether these inner qualities support the achievement of my goals and whether some of them, perhaps even familiar beliefs from childhood, no longer support me in accomplishing my life's purpose and vision. This clearer picture of who I am, what I believe and care about, how others perceive me, gives me valuable insight into where I really am in life, to where I could be, and to who and where I want to be.

Still, let's face it: It's often easier to remain in the dark, unclear and uncertain about my direction and goals. Plus, it seems to be safer (or at least more comfortable) to sleepwalk my way through life—which is why many people do it. It's safer, probably more frustrating and ultimately deeply discouraging. The natural way out of sleepwalking is simply waking up. The natural way out of unawareness is awareness, and with greater awareness, new opportunities for understanding and action emerge. Life becomes filled with and powered by possibility.

Later in this book we'll look at commonly held attitudes, habits and beliefs, how they can stand in the way of living an extraordinary life. We'll examine how you can transform your experience of life by simply becoming aware of those attitudes, habits and beliefs and how you can make new, more appropriate choices.

Once I have gained new insights through greater awareness, taking personal **Responsibility** enables me to produce tangible results in my life. This in turn, when combined with more effective communication, creates a virtuous circle leading to extraordinary personal results. The moment I stop blaming the circumstances of my life, attributing any lack of accomplishment to fate, or bad luck, or age or education, I begin seeing myself in the driver's seat of my own life. As I become aware of my choices and their impact on the world around me, I begin to realize that I am fundamentally responsible for the circumstances of my life. By accepting responsibility for "the way things are," I become more able to intentionally respond and create the results I want.

Character—which springs from the repeated willingness to accept responsibility for one's own life—is the source from which true self-respect is built. In my experience, that is absolutely true. Responsibility is at once powerful and empowering. It begins the instant I am willing to give up my victim point of view. Simply put, this requires I stop blaming others—my wife, parents, boss or even my dog, for the way my life is. More importantly (and the hardest of all for many of us), responsibility means I stop blaming myself.

Though it seems paradoxical, there is tremendous freedom in owning all of my results, even those I don't like and especially the ones I resist. Responsibility does not mean guilt, shame, obligation or burden. It means that I don't wait for someone or something outside of me to fix my life. I am the one making it happen.

A major part of this book will look at how even well educated, successful people subtly or not-so-subtly avoid responsibility, the prices we pay for doing that and how to transform our experience of living by simply taking 100% personal responsibility for our lives.

Once I am more aware and operating from personal responsibility, **Communication** becomes the critical consciousness and skill for living an extraordinary life. All of life's important results are generated by communication. If I communicate authentically, appropriately, and with passion, my communications will be effective in forging powerful relationships with others and amplifying the effectiveness of my choices in my personal life and in my career.

Communication is what holds every relationship together—in personal, corporate and community life—and it keeps things moving; it is the engine of accomplishment.

There are clear differences between people who accomplish extraordinary results and those who don't. Each one faces the real circumstances served up by life, each has hopes and dreams. The difference is that those who accomplish much lift their circumstances up to the level of their dreams through awareness, responsibility and communication; others lower their dreams to fit their circumstances. It follows that in everything I do, if I really want to succeed, I must articulate my needs and my vision in order to create the possibility for having my reality match my dreams. This demands that I master the art of communication.

John Donne said, "No man is an island, entire of himself; every man is a piece of the continent." It's a powerful statement, worthy of some reflection—and quite true. You can accomplish very little alone. Almost everything you want to be, do or have is dependent on your ability to communicate effectively with others. You may need to gain support for your ideas, generate a true partnership in service of a worthy goal or overcome opposition. That's assuming you are living a commitment to create an extraordinary life.

This book will reveal a unique approach to developing more than just communication techniques; you'll have the opportunity to adopt a entirely different way of being that will enhance your ability to communicate with power, passion and effectiveness.

If you sincerely want to escape from the ordinary, realize your dreams and live an extraordinary life, you need to master the tools of Awareness, Responsibility and Communication. That's not just my opinion, it's more like gravity; it's the way things are.

Around the beginning of the twentieth century, psychologist William James said, "The greatest discovery of my generation is that a human being can alter his life by altering his attitude of mind." One hundred years later at the dawn of a new millennium, James' statement is just as true and ultimately, that is much of what this book is about.

Welcome to the adventure of living an extraordinary life.

ORDINARY PEOPLE...

...own their limitations —live a version of "I am not enough"

...sleepwalk through life—they regularly miss life's wake up calls

...avoid feedback and resist any that appears in their lives

...are victims of people, circumstances, and even themselves

...fail as communicators or deny the importance of engaging others

EXTRAORDINARY PEOPLE...

...believe everything is possible

...have daily practices that lead to awareness, notice the impact of their choices on others and see the outcomes that are possible

...actively seek feedback

...are personally responsible for their lives—they avoid getting caught up in reasons and stories for why they don't have what they say they want

...communicate masterfully—they listen carefully, then are vocal and explicit concerning intentions and expectations

...acknowledge others for their feedback and contributions

...when confronted with inordinate stress or challenge, communicate... communicate...communicate...

~ 3 ~

YOU ALWAYS MAKE THE BEST CHOICE

*Everything can be taken from a man but one thing:
the last of the human freedoms—to choose one's attitude
in any set of circumstances, to choose one's own way.*

Dr. Viktor Frankl

Man's Search for Meaning

"Robert, here's something to think about: You always make the best choice." It was over thirty years ago and easily the dumbest statement I'd ever heard up to that point in my life. Worse, the friend who made it, Bill Schwartz, was trying to get me into some "life-changing" seminar he'd recently attended which was, as far as I could tell, based solely on that lunatic sentence.

"You always make the best choice." What nonsense. I immediately started listing in my head all the times I'd risked money and lost it, all the career moves that turned out to be dead ends, my divorce. How were all of those the best choices?

As much as I disagreed with his statement, I had to admit that there was something different about Bill, something positive and calm. He smiled more, and more naturally, and he seemed to listen more and talk less. There was warmth and intimacy I'd never experienced from him, and he simply would not engage in feeling sorry about my "victim" conversations, which infuriated the heck out of me. You know those conversations: the stories and excuses we all use to explain why we can't do something we want to do, the stories that explain how tough our lives have been, how much we've suffered.

The conversations that changed my life

Soon after that initially shocking introduction, Bill and another graduate of the seminar and friend, Larry Nelson, began creating opportunities to talk with me in a way I had never experienced. I don't recall every word; however the essence of these talks has stayed with me all these years. The conversations with Bill and Larry went something like this:

Robert, you know how much we value your friendship; however we have to tell you it's obvious that things are not going well for you. You seem to be in a constant state of anxiety. That's not surprising given that what you talk about is mostly your regret about things you've done or haven't done in the past, or your worries and doubts about the future. We know we might be putting our friendship on the line, but we're unwilling to stand back and do nothing while you are under this kind of stress. After we talk, if you want to tell us to go to hell, so be it. We're willing to risk that; however, for your own sake, please at least consider what we're going to say.

We'll begin by repeating what Bill said to you earlier. You always make the best choice. We know when you hear that, it might sound like nonsense and yet it's an idea that could transform your life. Until we took the seminar we've been telling you about, we both spent a lot time regretting choices we made years ago.

My reaction to these good friends was one of hidden interest and open resistance. Who were these guys to intrude on my carefully constructed yet essentially false image of having it all together? Bill went on to tell me:

On the second day of the seminar I've been telling you about, when the seminar leader told us, "You always make the best choice," I stood up and said, "I'm sorry but I think that's just bull. I don't know about anybody else in here, but I've sure as hell made some choices in my life that weren't the best."

I thought the facilitator might try to make me feel stupid, but he just said, "Tell me what happened to you, Bill."

So I spilled my guts. I told the group about the terrible mistake I'd made years earlier in choosing to quit my job and launch my own company. I told everybody how I was misled by the promoter of that business idea and how it turned out to be much more difficult than promised. I'd been forced to borrow against the equity in my home and put my relationship with my wife at risk. The long hours of trying to succeed were taking me away from involvement with my children's activities; and, my failure was embarrassing me with all my friends, especially the ones at the old job. I'd bragged about my bright new future, but the results were turning out to be nothing to brag about.

I told him he was right on target. I shared with the group how I'd been feeling depressed and guilty and angry with myself.

The facilitator listened carefully and then said, "You say you quit your job to start this new business, Bill. How come?"

I told him it was because after many years I was being intimidated and yelled at when I didn't meet my quotas. Plus, I felt taken for granted and given no recognition when I did create results. It was too bad, since I was about to be promoted. I've kicked myself lots of times for not being tougher, for not hanging in there and handling the pressure.

"And what about the new company you started? When you first launched it, what was it like?" the seminar leader asked.

I shared that it was great. I had learned so much and was treated with respect. My work was rewarded based on only my effort, for a change. And, I was much more committed since it is my company. However, the reality is, I'm failing.

He said, "Yes, we know it is failing now. At the time you decided quit your job and start the new business, did you know it would fail?"

Of course I didn't—I thought I would succeed and I told him so.

"What if your company were wildly successful?" he asked. "What would you be saying right now?"

I lit up like a light bulb and shared with the group that I'd feel like a genius for getting out of a situation I hated, taking control of my life and getting rich.

"So Bill," the facilitator said, "did you make the best choice in leaving your job to start your own business?"

I told him I thought I did, but now the company is failing and I'd lost so much money ….

He interrupted me. "Bill, let me ask you again. At that time, given what you knew then, without knowing what was going to happen in the future, did you make the best choice—among the choices that were actually available to you?"

I admitted that I did.

"Then don't you think it's time to stop beating yourself up, Bill?"

Robert, when he said that, a weight lifted off my shoulders that had been dragging me down for years. I suddenly felt free of the guilt and regret that I'd carried all that time. I realized that what he said was true: We always make the best choice. Not the best choice among all possible choices that we can imagine or fantasize, but the best choice among the choices actually available to us. We may look back, like I'd been doing for years, and with 20/20 hindsight wish we'd made a different choice. Yet at the time we make any choice, it is the best choice available to us; otherwise we'd choose something different.

So, if I always make the best choice, then instead of self-blame, I am simply responsible for all the results in my life. Not blame, simply responsible. This frees me to choose how I will respond to what happens in my life.

Robert, there is enormous personal power and increased feelings of self-worth when you take this kind of responsibility for your life. Believe me, it has profoundly changed my life in only a few months.

Larry chimed in with a quote from Winston Churchill: "The price of greatness is responsibility." Larry went on to say:

If you're not willing to be responsible, what's the alternative? I know only too well. Like me, you'll probably going to keep doing exactly what you've doing up to now, regretting the choices you've made and blaming yourself, others and circumstances. However, you already know what this approach to life brings you: gloom and guilt and the feeling of being a failure. By blaming, you make yourself into a victim, feeling powerless and out of control. You can't change the past, so why put energy into regret? It makes no sense, but so many of us do it anyway! Most people live their lives as victims, and an available choice is to not be one of them.

Robert, I know you don't like the outcomes of some of the choices you've made, but I guarantee you that those choices were the best available to you at the time you made them. You can regret what you did and beat yourself up, like Bill did for years, or you can take responsibility in its purest form and feel excited, empowered and positive.

Words alone can't explain how powerful it is to shift your relationship with life. In fact, that's why I want you to do the seminar. I turned my life around since attending and dozens of my fellow students are having similar breakthroughs.

These two great friends then gave me permission to either tell them to get lost or give their words some thought and meet later that week for a beer and more talk. (This was Milwaukee, Wisconsin—we did almost everything over a beer!) They stressed that they hoped it would be the latter choice, and, if I recall correctly, reminded me that they valued our friendship and didn't like to drink alone.

The journey begins

We had that beer together and Bill and Larry continued their enthusiastic recommendations that I should attend this seminar. Then, after resisting for a couple of months, into the seminar I went, dragging with me all the self-righteousness and defensiveness I could muster…which was a lot!

Though full of resentment at feeling "forced" to attend (still being a victim), deep down I must have known that my life could be better or different. Like most people, I didn't want to admit to myself or to anyone else that my life was less than perfect. Moreover, I did not relish the idea of change: I wanted my life to be different, but I didn't want to have to give up anything, or risk trying out new and unfamiliar behaviors. I secretly wished that someone would come along with a magic wand and painlessly solve all my problems (a belief that I was unaware of at the time).

The seminar turned out to be fantastic, perhaps the single most powerful experience of my life. After graduation I thanked Bill and Larry profusely for not giving up on me, and told them how the course had changed my life.

They looked at me incredulously. "Man, you still don't get it," Larry said. "The seminar didn't change your life, you did. The work you did in there was yours. Responsibility for the outcome is yours. The choice to participate—and have a powerful experience—was all yours. " He laughed. "See, getting used to living responsibly is not that easy."

I could only shake my head and laugh with him.

The subject is you…and first, a little about my journey

If I hear: I forget.
If I see: I remember.
If I do: I understand.

That extraordinary four-day seminar I took in the late nineteen-sixties was a major turning point in my life. The first thing I did after graduation was to enroll everyone I knew into the program. Friends, relatives and business colleagues had similar powerful, positive experiences, and our relationships became deeper and more rewarding. Before long I knew that making these seminars available to as many people as possible, was my passion, my life's work.

My active support attracted the attention of the company that presented the seminars (Mind Dynamics) and I was hired as President, learned the business and also went through their Instructor Training and Certification. After several years expanding MDI around the world, I launched my own training company, Lifespring, Inc., then sold it to the minority shareholders and pursued an opportunity to do the same thing in Japan.

Starting a business in Japan was the hardest thing I've ever done, and one of the most rewarding. Despite setback after setback, and being broke more often than I care to remember or even admit, my love and enthusiasm for the experience that people have in these seminars sustained me. Our success in Japan allowed us to promote our vision internationally, and over 500,000 men and women from 18 to 88 in Japan, Taiwan, Hong Kong, Australia and the USA shared the ARC seminar experience.

What I've learned about why this experience is such a powerful tool for people in unlocking their potential for joy and fulfillment, is the subject of the rest of this book.

I keep emphasizing the word "experience" because what gives our seminars their power, what makes them what they are, is the fact that they are experiential rather than didactic or intellectual or academic in nature.

Just a word or two on "experiential education," since it's become such a popular way to describe all sorts of nontraditional approaches to learning. "Experiential education" is more than just an educational methodology. It's true that, in contrast to traditional education, experiential learning involves learning by doing. Instead of listening to lectures, taking notes, memorizing facts and theories, and taking tests, students get involved physically, emotionally, and intellectually by participating in specially designed interactive exercises, games and processes. This makes learning about anything quicker and more fun, and helps you retain what you learn. To the greatest degree possible, this book is being written to encourage you to discover, to have some fun with your learning and to get around any intellectual defenses you normally utilize to block positive change.

The real difference between traditional and experiential learning, as we've developed it, is that experiential learning can generate an exploration, a discovery process, in which there is no single "right" answer. In our seminars and in this book, the subject matter is you. You're not challenged to learn our seven rules or ten principles about how to be successful in life. You'll have the opportunity to discover for yourself what really matters to you, what old habits of thinking and behaving keep you from having what you want, and where you want to go, what you want to accomplish from this moment on in your life. You'll have the chance to find your own answers, which may be very different than the answers for any other person.

And let's be clear: Our seminars and this book are not about fixing people. There is nothing to fix. Fixing implies that something is broken and needs to be mended. The average mentally healthy person with a few neuroses is not broken. Everyone can benefit from what has been described as a "return to wholeness," to the fun-loving, joyful, excited and focused person that you were during early childhood.

Do you "believe," or do you "know"?

I like to tell students: "The goal is not to prove that you are brilliant. The goal is to assist clients to discover that they are brilliant…" This is one of the reasons I favor experiential learning over explicit teaching. In experiential learning…(each participant) discovers relevant realities rather than hearing about them from an authority. Autonomy is strengthened in the very nature of the learning process.

Dr. Nathaniel Branden
The Six Pillars of Self-Esteem

There is a great personal certainty found in experiential learning. It is sometimes called "knowing," as opposed to "believing."

Certainty and knowledge, at least the kind that are useful in living an extraordinary life, can only be based on direct personal experience. For example, think of all the facts and theories you memorized in the hundreds of hours you spent in high school classrooms. If you're like most people, you probably don't remember most of what you "learned." (Thirty percent is the estimated national average in America.) However, if you ever learned to ride a bicycle, I'll bet you can get on one and ride today, even if it's been twenty years since the last time you rode. That's because you didn't read a book about how to ride a bicycle. You got on one and rode, with your Dad or somebody running beside you and picking you up when you fell down. Algebra is intellectual and can be forgotten. Riding a bike is part of you and never goes away.

In the same way, if you had never eaten a strawberry, I could try for the rest of my life to describe to you how a strawberry tastes. You might even believe me. However, when you eat a strawberry, then you "know." When people, through vivid life experiences or through our seminars or through this book, generate an experience, they "know"—in that same deep, certain sense—more about who they are, and how to authentically relate to others.

When the power and the passion of discovery come from within, then we "know" our insights are true and their value is arrived at from within, not externally imposed. That's because these realizations are not the views and opinions of someone else. Ideally, this kind of discovery takes place in a highly charged, emotional, even spiritual (and definitely not intellectual) environment. There can be no transformation, no awakening, no true personal growth, without the "here and now" experience of life, which involves every part of us, our bodies, minds, feelings and spirit, not just our intellect.

I'll leave the last word of this introduction, along with my personal thanks for his permission to use this, to the Nobel Prize-winning poet, Derek Walcott (my new favorite poet), who summarizes my feelings on self-knowledge and self-awareness so beautifully.

> "the time will come
> when, with elation,
> you will greet yourself arriving
> at your own door, in your own mirror,
> and each will smile at the other's welcome
> and say, sit here, eat.
>
> you will love again the stranger who was yourself
> give wine. give bread. give back your heart
> to itself, to the stranger who has loved you.
> all your life, whom you ignored
> for another, who knows you by heart.
>
> take down the love letters from the bookshelf,
> the photographs, the desperate notes,
> peel your own image from the mirror.
> sit. feast on life."
>
>   Derek Walcott

~ Part 2 ~

AWARENESS
*You are sleepwalking through life—
and how could you know it?*

~ 4 ~

Don't Believe Anything I Say

When the night has been too lonely
And the road has been too long
When you think that love is only
for the lucky and the strong.

Just remember, in the winter
far beneath the bitter snows
Lies the seed that with the sun's love
in the Spring becomes the rose.

"The Rose"
Performed by Bette Midler
Written by Amanda McBloom

It's the first morning of the Extraordinary Living Seminar. The seminar leader welcomes 150 participants and says, "You're going to be hearing a lot from me over the coming three days. Before we begin, the one thing I want you to remember is: Don't believe anything I say."

What, you might logically ask, is the point of attending a seminar in which you're not supposed to believe the instructor? A fair question, and one that occurs to every single person in the room.

As your facilitator in this book, I am going to say the same thing to you, the reader: Don't believe anything you read here. I invite you to question everything. If you are to gain significant value from this book, then the learning will come from and through you. This book is a chance for you to explore, a self-discovery process. If you simply take what I tell you as the truth, then what you'll get will be Robert White's discovery, not your self-discovery. While that might make me feel warm and wonderful, it will get you exactly nowhere.

The other reason our facilitators (and this author) tell people, "Don't believe anything I say," is that beliefs are conceptual, intellectual. And, if you stay at the intellectual level as you read this book, if you avoid getting emotionally involved, then it's unlikely that any real shift, any real transformation will take place in you. To get maximum value out of these pages, you need to be willing to jump in with both feet, be a bit vulnerable, take some personal risks and feel as well as think.

The key is take time out as you read these pages. Be willing to just stop and reflect. Pay attention to your reactions—especially the ones where you feel some anger or sadness or joy or fear—and examine your thoughts and feelings. Question what you have read. Does it relate to you personally, maybe touch a nerve, or cause you to think about something you've been trying to avoid or forget? Are you upset or sad or angry? If so, what does that feeling indicate to you? What could be leading you to react in a certain way? What are the underlying beliefs driving your behavior? In this context or in other situations, is that behavior getting you what you want in life, or getting in your way? Be willing to stop, look and consider making new, more effective life choices.

For example, if you started at the beginning and read the book in sequence, you already encountered a chapter entitled, "You Always Make the Best Choice." When you saw that heading, what was your reaction? Did you say to yourself: "What bull!?" Did you get angry as you disagreed? Did you start looking at all the bad choices you think you've made? Did you think that buying this book is one of those bad choices, and start being angry with me? What's that really about for you?

Be willing to take "time out" and look. Put the book down. Look at your reactions to each idea and the emotion you experience. What are you thinking, what are you feeling? Whatever comes up, ask yourself what it's about for you. "What is going on inside me that is generating my response?"

This book does not contain any universal truths—about anything. It simply asks you to take a few moments to look at your life and how you can have it work better, better in your relationship with family and friends, better in your workplace, better in your community and better in your relationship with the most important person in your life: you.

Based on the results from working with and observing over 500,000 people, I've learned that there are some choices and ways to live that are more effective than others. However, remember that you don't have to believe that either. Just read and question, and examine your own thoughts and feelings as you go.

Self-awareness and self-discovery are all about you alone answering the important questions in your life. You are unique, one-of-a-kind. There has never been anyone like you in the world before, and there never will be again. Only you can solve the problems created by you or presented to you in your life. Only you can decide to take control of your life, take it to new and exciting levels, and begin to see new possibilities.

I am simply your facilitator, your coach. Perhaps I'm an experienced coach who has good questions, some solid suggestions for expanding your experience of life, but as a coach, not a guru. You don't have to believe anything written here. The important thing is stop, consider, look inside, choose and then act.

Here's one exception, one thing you can believe: you *do* have the answers for living your own extraordinary life. That much I guarantee.

ORDINARY PEOPLE...

...believe so-called experts without critical examination of whether the ideas really resonate with their deeper selves

...stay stuck in their thinking and avoid, invalidate or ignore their body's feedback, their feelings and their intuitive or spiritual senses

...look for "the answer" and "the truth" from others, from outside of themselves

...always insist on "doing it myself"

...believe that "this is the way I am and I'll never/cannot change"

EXTRAORDINARY PEOPLE...

...question everything without cynicism

...have the courage to explore and discover their own truth

...honor their feelings, body sensations and spirit connection as well as their minds

...seek great coaches and consider their input

...expect an extraordinary life—with all the changes and surprises that come with it

~ 5 ~

THE MEANING OF LIFE

*If you want my final opinion on the mystery of life and
all that, I can give it to you in a nutshell. The universe is
like a safe to which there is a combination. But the
combination is locked up in the safe.*

Peter De Vries
Let Me Count the Ways

The meaning of life is a question that comes up when people begin to look deep within. Sigmund Freud answered the question with, "love and work." Not a bad answer—and I believe there's a lot more to it.

The closest I've come to a better answer than Freud's is a few paragraphs from Viktor Frankl's extraordinary book, *Man's Search for Meaning*:

> "To put the question in general terms would be comparable to the question posed to a chess champion: 'Tell me, Master, what is the best move in the world.'
>
> There is simply no such thing as the best or even a good move apart from a particular situation in a game and the particular personality of one's opponent. The same holds for human existence. One should not search for an abstract meaning of life. Everyone has his own specific vocation or mission in life to carry out, a concrete assignment which demands fulfillment. Therein he cannot be replaced, nor can his life be repeated. Thus, everyone's task is as unique as his specific opportunity to implement it.
>
> As each situation represents a challenge to man and presents a problem for him to solve, the question of the meaning of life may actually be reversed. Ultimately, man should not ask what the meaning of his life is, but rather he must recognize that it is he who is asked. In a word, each man is questioned by life; and he can only answer to life by answering for his own life; to life he can only respond by being responsible."

Responsible. We confront this challenge again and again. There seems to be no escaping the idea of personal responsibility as a crucial component in successful, even extraordinary living, and in finding the meaning of your life.

Like being thrown from an airplane

Try on this simile for life: Being born is like being thrown from an airplane at 30,000 feet—without a parachute. In between leaving the airplane and hitting the ground is your life. It's all the time you've got. This is not about being fatalistic. It is about dealing with our personal, absolute reality.

Now, you can't choose not to die, because that is inevitable. You can, however, choose your attitude about living. You can choose how you are going to experience those moments between leaving the airplane and hitting the ground. And that, after all, is what life is: your moment-to-moment experience. Your choice comes down to this: you can be in resistance to the reality of what life is, and make it one huge struggle, or you can accept life as it is and enjoy the ride.

Crazy? Not really. As you are falling through space, you could scream, "Oh, no, I'm going to die!!" and struggle and wail and curse gravity. Or, you could choose to accept "what is" and say, "Well, that's it. In a few minutes it will be all over. Meanwhile I am going to enjoy the fantastic view, the cold air rushing by me, the sensation of weightlessness, and seeing this incredible world from such a magnificent perspective. I am going to savor every moment—for the rest of my life."

Nobody knows when they're going to die. The rest of your life could be a few seconds, a week or twenty years. You don't know. These days, seventy or eighty years are common, but nothing's guaranteed.

So, why not live your life as if you only have a few minutes left, instead of wandering around in resistance to the way life is, laboring under the all-too-human hallucination that you will live forever?

> "You've got to sing like it ain't for the money
> Love, like you've never been hurt.
> Dance, dance, dance like nobody's watching.
> It's got to come from your heart if you want it to work."
>
> "Come From the Heart"
> Performed by Kathy Mattea,
> Lyrics by Susanna Clark
> and Richard Leigh

Being in resistance to "what is"—fighting gravity all the way down—is what can make life brutally demanding. Life is naturally much easier than we make it. Trees grow, flowers bloom, birds fly, sloths don't seem to do a heck of a lot, and I assume that platypuses do platypussy things—all without resistance to "what is." All species are designed to live that way: without resistance. Except humans. We complicate things and make life hard for ourselves by resisting life as it is. We try to change things over which we have no control. We want gravity to be different, for the immutable rules that govern our existence to somehow be suspended for us.

The "falling from an airplane" example is a choice of sheer terror all the way, or a decision to accept "what is" by choosing the joy of being alive. When I accept life as it is, not as I think it should be, then life starts to flow. Henry David Thoreau said, "The mass of men lead lives of quiet desperation." However, any experience of desperation is not due to external circumstances, it is due to internal choices. Simply put, it is a matter of attitude. And attitude determines everything—for your experience of the rest of your life.

Ordinary People…

…fail to—or refuse to—consider that there is meaning and purpose for their lives

…think and act as if they will live forever

…deny or resist the reality of life as we know it, of the immutable laws of the universe

Extraordinary People…

…accept and embrace responsibility for the gift of life, for their unique purpose in life

…live *here and now*

…dance like nobody's watching

~ 6 ~

A SMALL MATTER OF MIRACLES

I have observed the power of the watermelon seed. It has the power of drawing from the ground and through itself 200,000 times its own weight. When you can tell me how it takes this material and out of it colors an outside surface beyond the imitation of art, and then forms inside of it a white rind and within that again a red heart, thickly inlaid with black seeds, each one which in turn is capable of drawing through itself 200,000 times its own weight—when you can explain to me the mystery of a watermelon, you can ask me to explain the mystery of God.

William Jennings Bryan

On a TV show recently, the host was asking a group of people whether or not they believed in miracles. None said they did. The general consensus was that they were open-minded on the subject, but none of them had ever experienced an actual miracle. I found that disturbing, even frightening. How is it possible for us as human beings, who are probably one of the greatest miracles of all, to be so blind to our own miraculousness? (and if that's not officially a word, I just made it one, because the point can not be over-emphasized!).

Try to imagine this: Our own galaxy contains billions of planets and stars. It extends to around 20 million light years. Beyond that, astro-physicists tell us there are billions more galaxies…think of space, something which has no end. Infinite. Unimaginable. Within all of that, Earth. Tiny. Insignificant. One of uncountable trillions and trillions of stars and planets. Yet one which impossibly contains the even more impossible complex balance of forces, temperatures and elements to begin and to support life. How are we here? And why?

It is curious to me that even though we have developed incredible intellectual abilities, yet most of us are barely awake to our essential humanity, our bodies, thoughts, emotions and spirit. In the midst of all of this wonder, the absolute miracle of our existence, we sleepwalk, as if we are going to live forever, as if life were a dress rehearsal.

In terms of our awareness of "self" and the infinite wonder of our world, I could say we are as blind as bats, but that would be unfair—to bats. (Bats are a wonder. Nature's precursor to electronic radar, some bats can detect a mouse at thirty yards by emitting ultrasound waves of 200,000 cycles per second.)

You and I see ourselves as the intelligent form of life on earth, with scant regard for the intelligence in life itself and all its myriad forms, an intelligence that defies description. There are nearly two million officially classified species (estimates of the total number of species go as high as 100 million), from insects, plants, spiders, mammals, crustaceans and mollusks, to worms, fish, reptiles, jellyfish, coral, sponges, bacteria, fungi, algae and other organisms. Each species is amazingly different, and each has its own unique and ingenious strategy for survival and procreation. And as for the social organization and teamwork of the common yet magnificent ant…I don't even want to think about it.

No miracles? OK, let's you and I wrap our "intelligence" around the miracle of our existence as discussed in a few lines from *One World*, a book by quantum physicist Dr. John Polkinghorne, president of Queen's College, Cambridge:

> "In the early expanse of the universe there has to have been a close balance between the expansive energy (driving things apart) and the force of gravity (pulling things together). If expansion dominated then matter would fly apart too rapidly for condensation into galaxies and stars to take place. Nothing interesting could happen in such a thinly spread world. On the other hand, if gravity dominated, the world would collapse in on itself before there was time for the processes of life to get going.
>
> For us to be possible requires a balance between the effects of expansion and contraction, which at a very early epoch in the universe's history has to differ from equality by not more than 1 in 10 to the 60th power. The numerate will marvel at such a degree of accuracy. For the non-numerate I will borrow an illustration from Paul Davies of what that accuracy means. He points out that it is the same as aiming at a target an inch wide on the other side of the observable universe, twenty thousand million light years away, and hitting the mark."

You might want to give this some thought: How can something as immensely complicated as even the simplest organism have come into being all on its own? As Paul Davies says in his recent book, *The Fifth Miracle*:

> "Many wonderful phenomena have emerged in the universe...monstrous black holes weighing a billion suns that eat stars and spew forth jets of gas; neutron stars spinning a thousand times a second, their materials crushed to a billion tons per cubic centimeter; subatomic particles so elusive that they could penetrate light years of solid lead. Yet, amazing though these things may be, the phenomenon of life is more remarkable than all of them put together."

Enough. The point I want to make is simply this: If there are no miracles then we need to find another word for the existence of life—the existence of you and me—on earth. Call it a gift from spirit (God or god in whatever form that works for you), serendipity, happenstance or plain good fortune. I invite you to look at your life as if it were a miracle. To treat your life in any other way seems to me to be a terrible waste of your unique presence on this planet.

Questions, questions, questions
He who dies with the most toys is still dead.
Seen on a T-shirt

Most people generally believe that having all the answers—or appearing to—is the key to success, money, power and possessions. They rehearse situations, prepare cool and snappy replies and try at all times to be in control. They struggle and strain to appear in charge, important and affluent.

I believe life is about asking the right questions. If, at the end of your life, you are left with more questions than you began with, you will have achieved a richness of human experience that money and fame can't buy.

Questions. Like some ironic lines from Frank Sinatra in Pete Hamill's book, *Why Sinatra Matters*. "'You like people,' Sinatra said softly, 'and they die on you...And women...I don't know what the hell to make of them. Do you?' I said every day I knew less. 'Maybe that's what it's all about,' he said. 'Maybe all that happens is you grow older and you know less.'"

A good friend of mine once asked the great spiritual teacher, Krishnamurti, to define intelligence. He replied, "An endless curiosity." To be "endlessly curious" implies giving up "being right" and allowing ourselves to have more questions than answers. It invites us to live in awe of where we are at this moment.

Albert Einstein left no room for ambivalence when it came to the matter of miracles. He said, "There are only two ways to live your life. One is as though nothing is a miracle. The other is as though everything is a miracle."

Let me repeat: Each of us is unique, one-of-a-kind and, I believe, a miracle. You may see it differently. My invitation to you is to begin living every moment as though you are miraculous and deserve to live an extraordinary life. On an interim basis, fake it if you must and keep faking it until it's real to you. The gift you will be giving yourself is a lifelong journey of discovery and joy, one that is infinite and infinitely rewarding. Begin the journey. Today. This moment. Now.

ORDINARY PEOPLE...

...don't believe in miracles...including the miracle they are

...fail to acknowledge, to themselves and others, how totally unique they really are

...believe that having all the answers...is the answer

EXTRAORDINARY PEOPLE...

...believe in miracles and fully own the miracle of being that they are

...live life in wonderment, ask a lot of questions and are endlessly curious

...act now!

~ 7 ~

THE LAWS OF SCARCITY AND ABUNDANCE

Lord, won't you buy me a Mercedes-Benz,
My friends all drive Porsches,
I must make amends.

"Mercedes-Benz"
Performed by Janis Joplin
Written by Janis Joplin, Michael McClure and Bob Newirth

There are three types of people in the world, goes the old joke; those who can count, and those who can't. In truth, I think there might be just two types of people; those who live from a position of scarcity and those who live from a position of abundance.

People who live from abundance feel that there is more than enough of everything in the world to go around. More than enough money, food, work, material things, more than enough love. Why do they feel that way? Because they see that they themselves are enough. They are not dependent on external influences to make them feel more whole and complete.

People who live from a position of scarcity feel that there is never enough of anything. They are constantly thinking about the next thing they want to do, or have, or eat, or conquer. Bottom line, they are trying to fill an emptiness inside that can't be filled. The source of their emptiness is simple: they feel less than enough themselves. They feel incomplete, inadequate.

A young man in one of our seminars had made a fortune in California real estate. He was in his mid-thirties, bright, articulate, good looking. He enjoyed the usual trappings of wealth: the Ferrari, the model girlfriend, a townhouse in Los Angeles and a ski chalet in Vail. Perhaps "enjoyed" is the wrong word. In spite of his good looks and his expensive image, this guy looked miserable. I asked him why he'd come to the seminar.

"When I was 18," he said, "I promised myself I would be a millionaire by the time I was 30. Well, I made it before I was 29. I worked 16-hour days, never took a day off, never took a vacation. The day I sold my business, I said to myself, 'Now I can start enjoying life. Now I can be happy.' Then gradually, this black cloud descended on me. I didn't feel happy, I felt terrible. Now I just feel bored and numb. I came here because my life seems pointless. I came here to try to find some kind of meaning again. Otherwise I might as well jump off a tall building."

After ecstasy, the laundry

He was like a mountaineer who trained for years and finally climbed Mt. Everest. When asked how it felt, he replied, "There's nothing there." It can be much the same with all of our goals. We expect that a paradise of joy and bliss will accompany their attainment and transform our lives forever. Then nothing happens; after we reach our goals, we are the same, and so is everything else. As the Buddhist proverb goes, "After ecstasy, the laundry."

The young real estate tycoon's story represents a lesson for everyone. No amount of MORE made him content or happy with who he was. Each time he got MORE, what did he want? Even MORE. When he felt no satisfaction in reaching his latest goal, he'd raise the bar higher and higher. However, as long as he believed he was not enough, no amount of anything external to himself could possibly make any difference. The pursuit of MORE leads only to frustration and dissatisfaction. It is a self-defeating and never-ending journey. Like the donkey chasing the carrot on a stick, always tantalizingly out of reach, the pursuit of MORE generates activity, yet no sense of satisfaction or fulfillment.

Will MORE ever work to make you feel fulfilled and contented? Will that new boyfriend or girlfriend, that expensive vacation, or the purchase of piles of "stuff" you need to buy make you feel better about who you are? Think about it. Will you feel complete as soon as you get that new job? As soon as you make your first couple of million? As soon as you have that luxury speedboat? As soon as you meet the perfect mate? As soon as you get promoted? As soon as you win the local golf tournament? As soon as your divorce comes through? As soon as you retire? Yeah, right.

~ 8 ~

INSANITY IS NOT JUST FOR THE INSANE

One definition of insanity: Doing the same thing over and over again, and expecting different results.

Albert Einstein

(Paraphrased slightly)

Many people believe that insanity refers to psychosis or paranoia, or other forms of mental disorders. These relatively rare conditions may be forms of insanity, but there is another, more common and ultimately more dangerous form of insanity: Doing the same thing over and over and expecting a different outcome.

Crazy? Sure, yet that's what we do. We're geniuses at it. And if you keep making the same mistakes over and over again and don't know why, then welcome to the human race. Meanwhile, we look around for evidence to blame some bad luck, some unfortunate circumstance, instead of looking inside ourselves to identify the real cause of our repeated disappointments.

Why rats can be smarter than people

In this area, we humans can learn an important lesson from the study of rat behavior and rat psychology. Rats don't have the problem of self-sabotage. There are no rat shrinks counseling rat patients on how to free themselves from self-defeating behavior patterns. Rats have one purpose in life: to find the cheese and eat it. (In other words, to seek out and achieve what they really want.) Human beings are different. For us, unfortunately, something else is often more important than finding and having what we want and need to be fulfilled and happy—to free ourselves to lead extraordinary lives.

Don't buy it? Well, imagine you're a scientist studying rat behavior. You set up a maze with three tubes, Tube 1, Tube 2, and Tube 3. Down at the end of Tube 2, you put a nice, big piece of cheese. Then you let the rat go into the maze. What will the rat do? Sniff around Tube 1, Tube 2, and Tube 3, until he smells the cheese. And then what? The rat will follow his nose, go down Tube 2, find the cheese and eat it. Because that's a rat's purpose in life: to find the cheese and eat it.

What will happen if you keep putting the cheese in Tube 2 each time you let the rat go into the maze? Before long, the rat won't waste any time fooling around in Tube 1 or Tube 3. He'll run immediately to Tube 2, find the cheese and eat it.

And what if after a few dozen trials, you, the scientist, suddenly put the cheese in Tube 3 instead of Tube 2? What will the rat do? At first, of course, he'll run down Tube 2, expecting the cheese to be there, as usual. But if he doesn't find it in Tube 2, what will happen? Sooner or later, the rat will explore Tube 1 and Tube 3, and eventually he'll find the cheese and eat it.

What about human beings like you and me? Well, if you put our "cheese" of life (money, an intimate relationship, success, happiness) in Tube 2, we humans, with our large and complex brains, can find it even more quickly than a rat. We go through the learning curve in no time flat. And once we learn that the cheese is down Tube 2, we don't even glance at Tube 1 or Tube 3. We "know" where to find the cheese in life.

But what happens when you move the cheese from Tube 2 to Tube 3? What will we human beings do? Will we quickly and easily give up what we "know" and look down Tube 1 or Tube 3? Unfortunately, we probably won't.

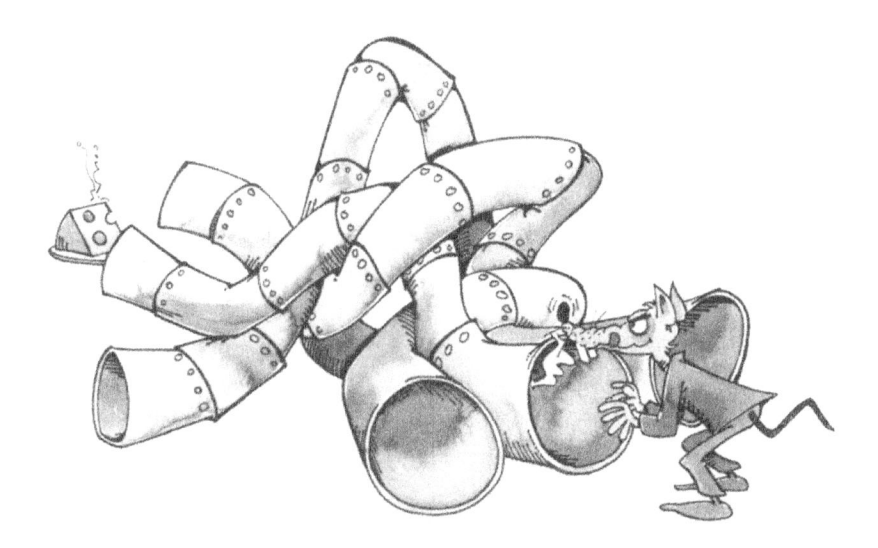

Awareness · 37

We'll keep going down Tube 2, over and over again, even though there's no cheese down that tube. Why? Remember, with our large and complex brains, our purpose in life is no longer simply to find the cheese and eat it. Much more important than having what we want is—being *right* about our beliefs, about what we've decided is true. Often we end up being right and missing out on the "cheese" in our life.

How does this work? Imagine that as I grow up, every night around the dinner table I hear my Dad say over and over, "You can't trust anybody. It's a dog eat dog world out there. The world is a cruel place, and people will try to cheat you and rob you every chance they get. You always have to be on guard. You've got to get them before they get you."

Will I, given that programming from an important person in my life, form a belief that people are untrustworthy? You bet. And imagine that, when I get my first job delivering newspapers at the age of 12, my boss leaves town without paying me my last month's wages. Will my belief be reinforced? Now I have evidence that people can't be trusted. And imagine that, at age 16, I lend my best friend $50 that I earned mowing lawns and moving furniture—and he never pays me back. My belief is on its way to becoming as certain as gravity: You can't trust anybody.

OK, so now I'm grown up, and I decide I want to go into the construction business, building houses, and I go looking for a partner to share the costs and the profits with me. What kind of a partner do I need? One I can trust, one who will be honest and keep his agreements.

However, with my belief that people are untrustworthy, what kind of a partner am I going to find, inevitably? Probably a partner I cannot trust. Somebody who, no matter how trustworthy they appear on the surface, sooner or later will lie to me, cheat me, rob me.

And when it happens, what will I say to myself? "I knew it, I knew it would happen. You can't trust anybody!" I'll get to be right. And what's more, unless I wake up and realize what is generating my behavior—what's the real source of this pattern in my life—I'll go out and repeat it. Over and over again. Unfortunately, what's included in this pattern is that I won't get the cheese in life. I won't get what I really want, the success, fulfillment, the joy that I'm actually seeking.

Mitigating the madness

A rooster crows only when he sees the light. Put him in the dark and he'll never crow. I have seen the light and I'm crowing.

Cassius Clay, later, Muhammad Ali
(after winning the world heavyweight boxing
title and revealing his conversion to Islam)

Self awareness is the first step to stopping this most common form of insanity. Self awareness allows us to begin to live "in the moment," to recognize our thoughts and feelings as they happen, to take time out to examine where we are heading. A plane leaving London for New York is set on a course, yet throughout the entire journey the plane is actually off course by a few degrees. There are dozens of factors, like headwinds or gravity which are constantly working to take it off course. The art of flying is an exercise in constant course correction. Today, a computer keeps track of the plane's altitude, direction, and speed, and constantly adjusts its course up or down, faster or slower, north or south, east or west. Without correction, the plane could easily end up in Boston or Washington, DC rather than New York.

As with the plane, so with our lives: Getting to the right destination requires a willingness to change direction many times. And making course corrections means knowing where the plane actually is. If our instruments are faulty—or if we pay no attention to the feedback we get—we can be badly mistaken about our current location. In order to get where we want to go, we need to be aware of where we are, and willing to make course corrections.

Successful people (by this I mean more than just "wealthy") use all the feedback in their environment—successes and failures, other people's reactions, their own thoughts and feelings—as a personal instrument panel that helps ensure a successful voyage and arrival at their chosen destinations. As Daniel Goleman rightly says, "The ability to monitor feelings moment-to-moment is crucial to insight and self-understanding…People with greater certainty about their feelings are better pilots of their lives."

Yet few of us pay attention to the feedback in our lives, to see what's working for us and what is not, let alone to notice the emotions we are experiencing moment-to-moment. Dr. Nathaniel Branden says in *The Six Pillars of Self-Esteem* :

> "In virtually all the great spiritual and philosophical traditions of the world, there appears some form of the idea that most human beings are sleepwalking through their own existence. Enlightenment is identified with waking up. Evolution and progress are identified with an expansion of consciousness.
>
> The higher the level of consciousness at which we operate, the more we live by explicit choice and the more naturally does integrity flow as a consequence."

Intellectually, we know for certain that we are on this planet for a very brief period, yet we tend to live we were going to live forever, as if there were no end to our life or to the lives of our friends and family. This not-so-subtle denial of death persists throughout our lives, unless we are lucky enough to get a dramatic, usually painful and invariably life-changing wake-up call.

The moments of our lives are ephemeral gifts, and we cannot afford to miss even one of them. Happily, you don't have to wait for a painful wake-up call. You can notice the miracle of your life right now. Awareness is a choice.

Awareness and three dollars...

These days, just awareness and three dollars will get you a cappuccino—no more. As vital as awareness is to the process of improving your life, to suddenly be awake and aware means nothing if you simply leave it at that.

Awareness only matters if it impacts my actions. When I sleepwalk through life, all is mundane, a safe routine. When I am awake and aware, living in the here and now, I see the world with new eyes. We often forget that every living thing we see—our friends and family, children, parents, pets, and all the animals and plants—they're all going to die sooner or later, and we don't know when. This moment is all we have, all we can count on. Being aware in this way means that when I come down the stairs to greet my wife or child at breakfast, it needs to be as if it were the first and only occasion, as if it had never happened before.

"Why does death so catch us by surprise, and why love? We still and always want waking. We should amass half dressed in long lines like tribesmen and shake gourds at each other; instead we watch television and miss the show."

Annie Dillard
The Writing Life

When I live in the moment, or more accurately, when I live as if this were the only moment I had, the daily round of home to office to home to weekend shopping to office is no longer tedious. I appreciate each moment for what it actually is—a new experience. Each day is filled with such moments, new and unique, totally different from the last, even if the activities in which I am engaged are exactly the same. Every 24 hours, I begin the day seeing myself and my world with a freshness that promotes true joy. My senses are alert to the sounds, sights and smells around me. I am fully alert to the moment of my existence. I am awake. I am aware. I am alive. I am.

A friend was working as a sales executive in England. He shared with me the story of one associate who was a total "routine freak." He did everything the same way every day. He asked how he could increase his income and was told to change everything in his routine and then change the change every day.

Get up at a different time daily, have a different breakfast, vary the route to work. It was even suggested he violate the very strong agreement he worked under to be "on time" everyday, to be late for work occasionally and learn to deal with the disapproval. My friend even helped his associate move his furniture and instructed him to keep moving it weekly. He cut the cable to the couple's only television as nightly TV watching was an essential part of the routine!

The result was dramatic—the associate's income increased exponentially. Of course, the really interesting ending to this story is that three years later, the associate was back to his routine and even his furniture had been returned to exactly the same location. His income had returned to its old level. He had temporarily changed his behavior and not his consciousness…so of course his behavior went back to its old pattern.

To make awareness of the moment an ongoing reality for yourself demands heightened alertness. You will need to keep working at it every day for it to be valuable. As you progress, you remain increasingly in the here and now; your experience will be sharper, cleaner, stronger and more alive. Feelings of contentment and joy will grow.

There is nothing "New Age" about the process of awareness, and neither is there any great secret to being more aware. You simply need to choose it, moment-to-moment. Again, it's simple, not necessarily easy, and you'll discover it is more than worth the effort.

ORDINARY PEOPLE...

...believe they are "not enough"

...live with a consciousness of scarcity

...stay stuck in dysfunctional patterns and are "right" about them

...are sleepwalking through life

EXTRAORDINARY PEOPLE...

...fully experience the gift they are

...live with a consciousness of abundance

...choose to let go of any belief or pattern that sabotages the accomplishment they desire

...choose and rigorously maintain a pragmatic, grounded and action-oriented awareness of themselves and their environment

~ 9 ~

INTENTION AND THE TITANIC

Most people live…in a very restricted circle of their potential being. They make very small use of a very small portion of their possible consciousness…much like a man who should get into the habit of using and moving only his little finger.

William James

The fantastic human brain operates on many levels, including the conscious and unconscious. At the conscious level we are aware of just a tiny percentage of our experience—our thoughts, feelings and physical sensations. More than 95 percent of our lives goes on unconsciously, below the level of our conscious awareness. In other words, we pretty much run on automatic pilot. Good thing, too, because if we didn't, we simply wouldn't be able to function.

Imagine a life in which you were totally conscious, aware of every sensation in your body, every emotion, every thought—with the need to consciously choose every action you took. Just getting out of bed in the morning would be impossible. Having to go through a checklist of infinite minutia would be exhausting. Just imagine: "Move appropriate muscles and open right eye, now left eye, blink right eye, blink left eye, blink both eyes in unison, bring left leg to the bedroom floor, take gravity into account and prepare to activate inner ear balance mechanism…" and all that while having to remember what to do next, and at the same time being flooded with memories of everything you ever learned and every single detail of your life since you were born.

To stop us from either going mad or being completely paralyzed, human beings are blessed with many unconscious functions that handle an infinite number of mundane tasks for us. Were it not for our non-conscious activities of the cerebellum, our hearts would not beat, our lungs would not breathe, our stomachs would not digest. Every unhappy event—and every ecstatic one too—would be playing in our minds, all at once. Our life experience would be incoherent, chaotic and overwhelming. Happily, we forget. Most of our bodily and cerebral functions run on "automatic pilot." And yet, this automatic pilot sometimes undermines us.

Picture an iceberg. The bulk of its power lies below the surface. The part of the iceberg that sunk the Titanic, for example, was not the 10 percent above the water; it was the 90 percent below the surface that did the damage.

For human beings, it is also often true that the 90 percent below the surface—our unconscious beliefs, attitudes and habits—sinks our fondest hopes and dreams. As we grow up, we draw conclusions, we form beliefs about ourselves, others and life itself. Many of these beliefs serve us well. For example, if you have a belief that diving off the top of a skyscraper will be bad for your health, that's clearly a useful belief that supports your well-being. What if, as you were growing up, you formed a belief that you can't trust men?

I remember clearly a woman (I'll call her Vivian) in one of our seminars who shared on the first night, after an exercise in honesty and trust, that she had said, "I trust you" to most of the women in the group, and "I don't trust you" to most of the men. When I asked her what she thought that was about, she said she'd been hurt by her ex-husband—and when I probed a little deeper, she hesitantly told us that he'd lied to her about having an affair with another woman.

"Well, now I understand why you said 'I don't trust you' to the men in the group," I said.

"That's not even the worst part," she said. "The worst part is that this is the second time it's happened to me. My first husband did the same thing." By now tears were rolling silently down her cheeks.

When I reminded Vivian that as adults, what we do is act out the beliefs we form in childhood, over and over again, to prove ourselves right, her whole story came pouring out. It was as if a dam had burst.

"I had no relationship at all with my Father," Vivian told us. "He left my Mom when I was less than two years old. He would send me cards on my birthday, and promise to come to see me, but he never did. My Mom raised me by herself."

"Maybe now you can see why you'd choose a man who would lie to you and break his promise to be faithful," I said. "Not once, but twice. In choosing both of these guys as your husband, what belief of yours did you get to be right about?"

"That you can't trust men to be there when you need them."

"That's the way it appears, doesn't it?" I said. "And remember what I said earlier: As human beings, we'd rather be right than be happy. In fact, we'll make ourselves miserable just to prove that we're right. So, it's time to wake up, Vivian. Time to start choosing what will nourish and fulfill you, instead of what will prove you right."

Less water, more ice

Becoming more aware isn't necessarily easy or comfortable. And I'll suggest to you that it's worth the hard work, worth the discomfort, many times over. As you become more aware, you have more choice about your behavior, and more ability to create the results you really want. Increasing your self-awareness means that more and more of who you are, and how you operate, moves from unconscious to conscious. It's like lowering the waterline to make more of the iceberg visible and accessible. You get to experience more and more of what is really driving your behavior: the beliefs about yourself and your world that either work well for you, or limit you, or prevent you from living the extraordinary life you want and deserve.

Let's look at it another way and again use that iceberg metaphor. Imagine that an iceberg is moving in a 3 mph current in one direction, and a 100 mph gale is blowing at the surface, pushing the iceberg in the opposite direction. Which direction will the iceberg go? It will of course be taken along inexorably by the ocean's current, pushing against the 90 percent of the iceberg that's below the waterline, slowed hardly at all by the gale howling above the water.

As human beings, our conscious intentions—the goals, desires, wants, wishes that we're aware of—are like the 100 mph gale. Our deep-rooted beliefs, attitudes and habitual behaviors are symbolized by the irresistible push of the ocean current against the hidden 90%. It doesn't matter a damn what my conscious desires may be; if my unconscious beliefs or habits are in conflict with them, my unconscious beliefs will prevail. Unlike the rat who always finds the cheese, our unconscious beliefs and habits keep taking us down the same tube again and again. Because we're not aware of what's actually generating the results in our lives, we keep feeling surprised and betrayed when we find there is no cheese down the same old tube.

Fat or thin, you are the weight you intend to be

Let's look at a concrete example that many of you will be able to relate to: body weight. Perhaps you are among the millions of people who say to themselves, "I'm overweight. I really need to lose a few pounds." (According to statistics, over half the people in the Western world are on some kind of diet at any one time.) If you are, you're a living, breathing example of how the 10 percent of the iceberg may be blown in one direction, while the 90 percent moves irresistibly in exactly the opposite direction. Think about it. At the 10 percent level, the level of your conscious goals, you say to yourself: "It's my intention to weigh X (whatever you consider the right weight for yourself)." But at the 90 percent level, the level of your unconscious beliefs and habits, you have a different intention—one which conflicts with your conscious plans.

Now, I realize that you probably don't sit around asking yourself: "What's my intention in being overweight?" If you're like most people, you blame being overweight on something. Maybe you blame it on all the traveling you've been doing, which forces you to eat out at restaurants that serve fattening foods and prevents you from exercising. Or maybe you blame it on your slow metabolism that you inherited from your mother, who was always overweight. Or the fact that you chose the wrong diet plan, since even though you lost weight, as soon as you went off the diet you gained it back again. Or maybe you blame yourself. Maybe you say: "I was just born with no will power when it comes to food—there's nothing I can do about it."

Understanding your true intention

Here's a different point of view: Your body weight is not an accident, and not determined by circumstances or your environment—though the environment you choose to put yourself in can certainly support you or deter you from being the weight you want to be. Your body weight (like all the results in your life) is the product of your true intention. By "true intention," I mean both your conscious goals and desires, and your unconscious wants and needs—like the need to be right about your beliefs, or the desire to protect yourself from getting hurt, or the need to stay in control at all costs.

Here's the bold statement: "You weigh exactly the amount it is your intention to weigh, not a pound more or less."

When I made this statement in one of our seminars, I noticed a big man (I'll call him Sam) in the front row shaking his head from side to side. I couldn't tell if he was disagreeing with me or bewildered so I asked him what was going on. He stood up and said that he agreed with what I was saying, but he couldn't understand how it could be his intention to weigh as much as he did. "It just doesn't make sense," he said.

When I asked Sam how much he weighed, he told us 235 pounds, which was at least 35 pounds overweight, by his standards. And when I asked him if he'd ever tried to lose those 35 pounds, he said he'd gone on dozens of different diets—but he always gained the weight back.

"So at the conscious level, Sam, you say to yourself: 'My intention is to lose 35 pounds.' At the unconscious level, the 90 percent hidden level of the iceberg, what appears to be your intention?"

"To weigh 235 pounds, apparently," he said.

"That's right!" I said. "To weigh exactly what you weigh! How do you know that's your actual intention?"

He thought for a minute. "If I accept what you say, I guess I know it because that's how much I actually weigh."

"Right again, from my point of view. The results don't lie. The results always reveal what our real intentions are. So, let me ask you, Sam: What's your intention in being 35 pounds overweight?"

When Sam said that he really didn't know, I asked him to consider it from a different angle. What might be the advantage, I asked, the hidden benefit, in weighing 35 pounds more than he consciously wanted to.

"The advantage?" he said. "I can't imagine what it could be. When I look in the mirror, I hate myself for not having the will power to lose weight."

So I asked Sam if he'd always been 35 pounds overweight. And he told us that it was only after he'd gotten married that weight became a problem—that he'd put on almost 50 pounds in his first two years of married life.

"What was going on during those first years of your marriage?" I asked.

"Well," he said, "I married my wife my senior year of college. We had to get married, because she was pregnant. As soon as I graduated, I had to get a job and support her, because she couldn't work. In fact, she had to quit school in her sophomore year."

"And how did you feel, just out of college, with all that responsibility, going out to get your first job?" I asked.

"I was afraid," he said. "Afraid I was going to fail."

"And when you started working," I asked, "How did you feel around the other people on the job?"

"Like a kid," he said. "I was 22, but I looked like I was 16. Everybody called me 'Sammy.' Or just 'boy.'"

"And what does it seem your intention was in gaining that weight in the first year after you were married—even though maybe you weren't aware of it at the time?"

"To be bigger," he said slowly. "So people wouldn't push me around. And to look older. I remember after I gained weight thinking that I didn't look like I was 16 any more."

"Seems likely, doesn't it?" I said. "Tell me this, Sam: Are you that inexperienced, baby-faced kid any more?"

"No," he said, "I'm not."

"Then maybe it's time to make a new, conscious choice about your weight. A choice that supports you in feeling good about yourself, a choice that allows you to feel that you have integrity."

That's Sam's story. What about you? If you're overweight (or underweight), what's the hidden benefit for you? Is it:

- To avoid being hurt in another relationship?
- To avoid the risk of finding out whether or not men (or women) find you attractive?

- To be right about your belief that you're not attractive, not worthy, not lovable?
- To punish yourself for something you did that you think was wrong?
- To prove that you're in control, that nobody can tell you what to do with your body?
- To be right about your belief that men (or women) can't be trusted?
- To give yourself excuses for mediocrity, excuses for taking it easy, for not challenging yourself?
- To be right about your belief that you have no will-power, no self-control?

We imagine that we're safe, that by being overweight (or underweight) in some way we're protected from hurt. Are we really? Sure, we stay safe and keep the pain at a low level. Simultaneously we may prevent ourselves the chance to enjoy loving and rewarding relationships, or a truly fulfilling career, or real self-esteem.

The alternative is to crawl out of my cave and meet life head-on. By doing that, aren't I more likely to get my heart broken and be hurt again? Sure, that possibility always exists. However, I am already in pain, alone and safe in my hideaway. If I stick my head out, there is a chance of pain, but there is also a chance of joy and fulfillment. Staying where I am, stuck in my limiting beliefs about myself and others, only guarantees long-term pain.

ORDINARY PEOPLE...

...fail to pay attention to their own deeper levels of consciousness —their feelings and core beliefs

...often have multiple unconscious self-limiting beliefs

...believe in their limitations and even defend them vigorously

...trust in luck or circumstances

EXTRAORDINARY PEOPLE...

...are in a never-ending process of discovery about their inner selves—their patterns, why they do what they do

...they have a sense of their belief system and how those beliefs translate into behaviors

...seek feedback, confront and deal with any self-limiting beliefs

~ 10 ~

YOUR UNCOMFORTABLE COMFORT ZONE

To myself, I seem to have been only like a boy playing on the seashore, diverting myself now and then finding a smoother pebble or a prettier shell than the ordinary, whilst the great ocean of truth lay all undiscovered before me.
Sir Isaac Newton

In the heating and air conditioning business, they've come up with a descriptive term that is also a powerful metaphor for risk avoidance. The area on the thermostat in which neither heating nor cooling must operate—around 72 degrees—is called the "comfort zone." It's also known as the "dead zone."

All of us have areas of life that we will not enter and boundaries we will not move beyond. For even the most adventurous of us, that is perfectly normal. It could be the high altitude mountaineer who is unwilling to ask a woman out to dinner. Or the cool stunt man who risks his neck every day and yet is terrified to speak in front of a group. (Surveys consistently show that public speaking is the biggest single fear of most people—death comes in at fifth place on the list.)

Our comfort zones are natural, and they help us survive, yet they are misnamed because they are not truly comfortable. More accurately, they are just "habit zones." The big problem with living in one's comfort zone is that we know at some level there is more to life than our present experience. The trouble is, we don't want to risk going out and getting that something "more." By not going for it, by not jumping out of our comfort zone, we create a chronic low level of frustration, mediocrity and discomfort. Staying firmly in our safe routines—our so-called comfort zone—is not all it's cracked up to be.

Think about it. If life in your comfort zone is safe but often tedious, and if you feel there could be a lot more to life if you could just go for it, then what is holding you back? If you are living in a free society, not in prison or dire poverty, if you are not shackled in chains and are of reasonable intelligence, then what is preventing you from breaking out of your comfort zone and doing what you really want to do? If you're like most people, what you say to yourself is: "I don't have enough money," or "My partner won't approve," or "It's too late to start," or any of a thousand other excuses.

In fact, what is actually getting in the way of you jumping out of your comfort zone? From my experience, it's only one thing: fear of risking. Fear based on limiting beliefs.

When we use the term "limiting beliefs," it sounds rather abstract and artificial, like some kind of conceptual barrier. As a result, you may imagine that surpassing or going beyond your limiting beliefs is an easy task, requiring merely a little thought and reflection. Nothing could be further from the truth.

The life or death stuff called beliefs

Imagine that you're three or four years old, and you wake up in the middle of the night. It's dark, and you're alone. You call out for your mother, but no one answers. You start to cry, but still no one comes. You begin to scream and wail, but it's pitch-dark and you're all alone and no one comes to pick you up. You're gripped by fear, the fear that you've been abandoned, that no one will ever come. You rock yourself to sleep. When you wake up in the morning, your mother's there. You had no way of knowing that she had just gone down the hall for a few minutes to start some laundry. If this kind of thing happens repeatedly to you as a child, what's the belief you're likely to form? Something like: "No one, not even people who say they love me, will come when I need them. I can only depend on myself."

How serious is this belief you formed on limited information? It's a matter of life and death. And what kind of fear is associated with our bottom-line limiting beliefs? The fear of death, the fear of not surviving. That's why breaking out of our comfort zone can actually seem life-threatening. That's why it invariably takes courage to break out of our comfort zone. We have no way of knowing what's on the other side or whether we will succeed. (What's really on the other side is excitement, enrichment and growth—and, before long, another comfort zone to explore.)

Do you have your beliefs, or do your beliefs have you?

*To doubt everything or to believe everything are
two equally convenient solutions; both dispense
with the necessity of reflection.*
Jules Henri Poincare

Sometimes, in the middle of one of our seminars, the facilitator will suddenly ask people sitting in a few random rows to stand up. "All right," she says, "I want all of you to come up on the stage and, one at a time, tell the class the most embarrassing experience of your life." She pauses for about 10 seconds of stunned silence, and says, "It's OK—I was only joking to make a point. Here's what I want you to share: What physical reactions did you experience just now?"

Feedback will typically range from a rapidly pounding heart, sweaty palms and confusion, to trembling legs, a stomachache, and tight muscles. In other words, their primal "fight or flight" survival instinct had been engaged.

If a hungry lion suddenly ran into the room, those symptoms would be appropriate. Physiologically, your body is preparing to fight or run. Sweaty palms and armpits are your body's way of cooling you down in preparation to run. Digestion ceases and your stomach knots, preparing to apply all of your energy to winning this life-threatening challenge. Your face turns white, your hands and feet feel cold—nature's way of taking valuable blood from the extremities and sending it to the areas of your body that will need greater strength for combat or speed. All of these physical reactions have evolved as a means of survival.

Did a hungry lion come into the room in our little sharing example? No. The facilitator only said a few words. Yet people had exactly the same reactions as if a lion was at their throats. So what had actually happened?

First, the facilitator's out-of-the-blue instruction evoked fear in most students: fear of embarrassment, fear of speaking in front of a large audience, and fear that strangers might get to see inside me and find out that I am not as strong and self-assured and intelligent as I pretend to be. These fears are not real, of course. They're based on my limiting beliefs: the belief that—

underneath the image I try to project in public—I am unattractive or stupid. Or the belief that if I speak in front of people, I'll make some kind of mistake and everybody will judge me, laugh at me and look down on me. Or the most irrational, wasteful and destructive belief of all: that the person I really am behind my public image is not worth knowing.

What this exercise demonstrates is how much our beliefs have influenced our behavior since we were little children. Back then we were spontaneous, joyful, honest and fully alive. We had no trouble speaking in front of people. We didn't worry about being embarrassed, showing everyone who we were. Over time, all that changed. Many of us were bombarded with negative messages from our parents, brothers and sisters, teachers and friends, so that we developed a less than ideal self-image and a set of limiting beliefs that run our lives.

Some of these beliefs are appropriate: they protect and sustain us. They help us live and succeed. "Don't run out in the street without looking both ways" is a limiting belief, but a critical one for people who live in cities. "Don't go to bed without brushing your teeth" is a nuisance if I am a child, but it supports oral hygiene and my long-term health. Both beliefs—and the behavioral habits they support—are important for social animals who want to survive and flourish.

On the other hand, beliefs like, "I'm stupid," or "If I speak in front of people I'll look foolish," or "the real me is no good," keep us paralyzed, self-doubting, stuck in our uncomfortable comfort zone.

Each of us developed a set of limiting beliefs because, at the time, they seemed absolutely necessary to our survival. And—in a way—it worked: We're still alive. That was then and this is now.

Some beliefs are no longer relevant to our lives. In fact, they may be exactly the things that prevent us from expanding ourselves and accomplishing what we want.

Beliefs + H_2O = You

It has been said that human beings may be little more than water and a set of beliefs.

As human beings, our behavior is consistent with our inner beliefs. No matter how strange or inconsistent or even self-defeating a person's behavior may appear to an outside observer, it is always in synch with his belief system.

Observe someone's behavior, and you can determine the beliefs that generate it.

That we are all a product of our beliefs is not news. Everyone from Buddha and Jesus to Goethe and Shakespeare has had something to say on the subject. The Old Testament, in Proverbs 23:7, refers to it: "As a man thinketh in his heart, so is he." And early this century, Henry Ford made his contribution to the literature on beliefs with his now famous: "If you think you can, or you think you can't, you're probably right."

Each of us has deeply ingrained beliefs, a set of largely unconscious basic values which we derive from our culture, our family, and our experience in growing up. As children, however, we often misperceive and misinterpret what is said or happens around us. We form beliefs that are highly inaccurate or inappropriate given the reality presented. Or, to put it another way, we have lots of beliefs that we, well…simply made up. I made up mine, and you did the same. It may come as a severe shock if you haven't given much thought to this subject before—but our precious, cast-in-stone, "objective" beliefs are often totally in contrast to any reality. Or, more accurately, they are our perception of reality, rather than reality itself. The question we need to ask is, are our beliefs really true, or just our beliefs? It is important that we see the distinction—our ability to live a truly extraordinary life may depend on it.

Don't confuse me with the facts

*If nobody ever said anything unless he knew what he
was talking about, a ghastly hush would descend upon the earth.*
Sir Alan Herbert

Sometimes two or three brothers or sisters who grew up together in the same household come to one of our seminars—and it's always revealing and instructive when they begin comparing notes on what they remember from childhood.

Several years ago a man in his mid-thirties shared with the group about his memories of a Christmas when he was 10 years old. He told us how his dad had been promising for months to buy him a new bicycle. They had even gone to the bicycle store, looked at all the bikes, and picked one out. His heart was set on it, he told us, and at that point there was nothing that seemed more important in life than that new bicycle. Then, a few weeks before Christmas, his dad lost his job. On Christmas morning, there was no new bicycle. He hated his dad, he said, for breaking his promise. He ended by saying: "It might sound like a little thing now, only a bicycle, but at the time I felt lied to and betrayed. That was the worst Christmas I can remember."

Then his sister stood up. "Listening to you," she said to her brother, "I can hardly believe we come from the same family. I remember that Christmas when Dad lost his job, and it was the best Christmas of my whole childhood. That was the year we didn't have all those stupid presents that nobody wanted anyway, when we didn't have to spend Christmas morning opening packages and pretending to like stuff we didn't even want. That was the year we all sang Christmas carols together, and Dad read books to us, and we all went on that long walk in the snow—don't you remember? We were all together and it was wonderful."

Her brother only looked puzzled and shook his head. "I don't remember any of that," he said. All I remember is going outside in the snow by myself and throwing snowballs at a tree so nobody would see me crying."

Same events—totally different experiences. What "really" happened? No one will ever know. In fact, it's a meaningless question. All we have, each one of us, is our experience, and our experience is always filtered by our beliefs and expectations. And we form those beliefs, not based on objective reality—on what "really" happened—but on our own perception of what happened.

If you can see this distinction—that your beliefs are based on personal experience and perception, not objective reality—the next question becomes: Do you really want your limiting beliefs to run your life? Do you really want to your success, your happiness, to be controlled by decisions you made, often years ago, about yourself, other people, and your world? If you are like most people, what you want is to be in control of your life, to change the beliefs that are holding you back, to accomplish more of your dreams and live an extraordinary life.

The first step in this process, as I've said, is to become aware of the beliefs that are holding you back. As you become more aware, the next step is to muster the courage and commitment to pay the price necessary to give up any limiting beliefs.

Pay the price, you say? What price? I want to get rid of those limiting beliefs, as quickly as possible. Well, maybe. Then again, maybe not. Getting rid of limiting beliefs seems to be a little different than throwing away an old pair of shoes that have grown uncomfortable. It seems paradoxical, but in fact you and I often cling to our limiting beliefs, no matter what they cost us in terms of aliveness and accomplishment.

You are running a protection racket

The problem is that, while they hold us back, limiting beliefs also protect us. They protect us from having to risk, from having to try things where the outcome is uncertain and we might fail. And (as we know from past experience) failure hurts. So we hold on to our limiting beliefs. It's a self-perpetuating, vicious cycle.

I've worked with thousands of people in our seminars and it's clear that many of us, as a result of our childhood experiences, end up with a limiting belief that sounds something like: "If I open myself up to others, if I express who I really am, I'll be rejected." If you don't operate from some form of this limiting belief, and feel no need to present an image to the world in order to protect yourself, consider yourself fortunate.

If you do have this limiting belief, what's the protection racket it allows you to run? Well, for one thing, it allows you to be shy (if you're a woman) or silent and unexpressive (if you're a big, strong macho man). You have a great excuse for not taking the risk of expressing yourself, for withholding what you think and feel—which is obviously much safer than speaking up. You also have a great alibi for not becoming too vulnerable with other people in relationships. You can stay inside your shell, where it's safe, because (you think) if you open up, you'll just be rejected anyway. And on and on. It's a racket—a game in which my behavior reinforces my beliefs and my beliefs reinforce my behavior in an endless negative cycle of self-fulfilling prophecy.

People, however, are not dumb—and this includes you and me. We hang onto our beliefs because we think they serve us—because, as painful or boring as it may be to live within our limitations, at some level we're convinced that it would be worse if we gave them up.

If I believe that because I am only five feet three, I can never have a loving relationship, I'm blind to the fact that there are many women who would be glad to be in a relationship with a man who is five feet three. In my loneliness and self-pity, I don't even see them. Why do I stick with this self-limiting belief? Simple. It protects me: I don't have to risk rejection from women who may not want a relationship. And in my mind, that possible rejection is worse than the constant pain of loneliness and unworthiness I've got every day of my life. And because I make no effort to meet women, I have no relationship.

ORDINARY PEOPLE...

...live fearful lives of safe routines—in their comfort zone

...conclude that it is more important to stay safe than to actually get what they want in life

EXTRAORDINARY PEOPLE...

...take risks and break out of their comfort zone

...often live courageously by confronting and transcending limiting beliefs

~ 11 ~

THE MOST COMMON SELF-LIMITING BELIEF IN THE WORLD: "I AM NOT ENOUGH"

It is absolute perfection and virtually divine to know how to enjoy our being rightfully. We seek other conditions because we do not understand the use of our own, and go outside ourselves because we do not know what it is like inside.

Montaigne, 1588
From "Of Experience"

Human beings have used their incredible abilities to develop a staggering array of limiting beliefs, justifications and excuses for every occasion. What a waste! They range from, "Life is hard" and "I'm restricted by my physical condition," to "Men are better than women," "Women are better than men," "I had a terrible upbringing," "I'm too fat," "I'm too thin," and millions more. There is an excuse for every occasion.

As we saw in the last section, unless we are extremely fortunate, the strongest message we receive while we're growing up is this: "Who you are is not OK." The result is that, despite my desperate attempts at academic or sporting achievements, fame, status, power, position and material wealth, I will still feel inadequate *no matter what I accomplish* because I am operating from the basic and flawed belief that "I am not enough." No amount of outward success can ever fill that void.

Here are some common versions of the "I'm not enough" belief:

> I have nothing to contribute.
> I'm not important.
> I'm a failure.
> I don't deserve to have the best.
> I'm not lovable.
> Everyone knows more than me.
> I can't because I'm not creative.
> I can't because I'm too shy.
> I can't because I'm lazy.
> I can't because I'm afraid.

I can't because I'm not strong enough.
I can't because I'm not assertive.
I'm too young.
I'm too old.
My nose or ass or hips or ??? are too big.
My breasts or penis or ??? are too small.
I'm unattractive.
People always rip me off.
I can't trust men.
I can't trust women.
I can't be happy.
I can't talk to people.
I can't because I didn't go to college.
I can't because I'm just like my father/mother.
I can't because I'm not like my father or mother or Julia Roberts or Mel Gibson.
There's not enough time.
Life is a never-ending struggle.
I'll never have enough money.
I can't trust myself.
People are all bad.
People are all better than me.

I could go on with this list for another ten pages. I think you get the point. We human beings are infinitely creative in the ways we limit our lives. There can be no escape from this self-destructive cycle, until I choose to dump my basic belief that I am not enough and acknowledge the gift that I am: to myself, to my friends and family, to my colleagues and to my community. Then and only then, will my experience of life change.

The train always follows the tracks

A cabdriver sang his songs to me, in New York...One long song he sang twice; it was the only dull one. I said, "You already sang that one; let's sing something else." And he said, "You don't know how long it took me to get that one together."

Annie Dillard
The Writing Life

I love that quote–it's like Annie Dillard has been following me around and knows *my* life first hand.

As you and I both know, people are not stupid. I'm sure you know when your life is not working the way you want it to. That's what complaining is all about. Often we are even aware of an urgent need to do something different, but we want to remain comfortable as it happens. We want to weigh less yet eat as much and not exercise. We want to be successful at business, but not try anything where we might fail. We want a great relationship with our partner, but we don't want to be 100 percent committed. You and I want various results to occur effortlessly, without any discomfort, without work, without—change. We imagine the impossible: changing our results without changing our actions, and changing our actions without changing our beliefs.

Perhaps you are already able to see that life does not work that way, that there is no gain without some kind of effort or pain. One thing is certain: If you always do what you've always done, you'll always get what you always got.

Until you begin to be aware of and to take the risk of changing the limiting beliefs you hold—the ones that don't support your growth and success—you will surely continue to get the same results you've always had.

Scott's story

*I choose to value myself, to treat myself with respect,
to stand up for my right to exist.*

Nathaniel Branden
from *The Six Pillars of Self Esteem*

Because he has such a fascinating and rich background as a writer, traveler and adventurer, I asked a British graduate, Scott, if I might tell a little about how he came to our seminars, and what he experienced. Like the other personal stories in this book, it would be told under an assumed name. "Robert," he said, in his East London twang, "How about we just tell the entire bloody thing—exactly like it is?"

I leapt at the opportunity. With equal and undignified haste, I also later asked him to write it himself. So here it is, "the entire bloody thing," Scott's story:

> "Some people seem to learn life's lessons with a minimum of hurt. Others seem to learn them only after they have been right down the toilet emotionally. I think most people go

through life suffering a low level of continuous pain, learning very little, numb, deadening themselves with alcohol or some other form of avoidance, a kind of a living death. I am a down-the-toilet type.

"The question you might ask is the question many people have asked over the years. Everyone, that is, except me. Why would someone who was talented and well-liked beat himself up psychologically, to the point where he landed in hospital with depression and almost died? How could that happen? And what could have caused it?

"It's an excellent question. My doctor gave me an answer, but at the time it meant nothing to me. In fact, I didn't even know what he was talking about when he told me I had low self worth and hated myself. We were at lunch at the exclusive Garrick Club in Covent Garden when he matter-of-factly gave me that diagnosis. 'Look around,' he added. 'If I told you the names of some of the top executives in here that I'm treating for the same thing as you, you probably wouldn't believe it. It's what drives many of them. They feel they are never good enough, never accomplishing enough, so they're out there working harder and harder to produce better and better results. Their shareholders must love them, but that won't help them to love themselves.'

"I had plenty of good reasons to hate myself, or so I imagined. I'd left school at age 15, and because I hadn't gone to college, and spent 10 years bumming around the world, I felt like an imposter. What was an uneducated guy like me doing running my own company, writing for leading newspapers, and organizing successful adventures all over the world? What was a bum like me doing with friends who were highly educated, successful and wealthy? That was just part of it. I'd devoted much of my life to chasing women, and never being satisfied with any of them. I just moved from one to another looking for someone, something to make me feel better. It didn't work. I felt completely worthless, empty. Why?

(Editorial Note from your author: It's time to invoke my favorite questions from dear friend and teacher, the late Dr. John Jones: "What's so? So what? Now what?")

"In one of the advanced seminars I discovered that 'why' I felt the way I felt really didn't matter. As I heard many times in the seminars that after one gets 'what's so,' the next step is to get 'so what' and 'now what?' And at the same time, I found out more than enough about the origins of my low self-esteem to get me clear. It was during a simple exercise about our parents. We were asked to stand up and imitate the physical and emotional traits we most remembered about our father when we were growing up. Before I knew what was happening, I shot out of my chair with my arm raised high and my hand open, as if I was about to hit someone. That was it! I was brought up under the threat of physical violence. The fact that it was seldom carried out meant nothing.

"As a little kid, I had made an unconscious decision that if my own father would threaten to hit me, then I must not be worth much. With these kinds of emotional scars buried but not healed, I devoted myself to collecting evidence that I was no good, that I was deserving of my own hatred. In order to be right, I compared what I viewed as my mediocrity as a writer with everyone from Sartre to Shakespeare, and got angry because I was not Albert Einstein, Reinhold Messner or Bob Dylan.

"Do I hate my father for that? Not at all. Through the seminars I found out that he had done to me exactly what his parents had done to him. That was all he knew. If he'd known how to be a better father, then he would have. I was able to forgive him on that basis.

"And I began to love and appreciate who I am, as the John Denver song says, to appreciate 'The Gift You Are.' With that greatly increased self-acceptance and self-love, I stopped (at least most of the time) comparing myself to others. I stopped chasing women because I had looked deeply inside and discovered that I no longer needed to look to someone else to feel content and fulfilled.

As positive as these changes are, they did not happen overnight. I had to work on it. I am still working on it, and I hope and expect that I always will be."

Scott

A Flying leap into the void

Come to the edge, he said.
They said: We are afraid.
Come to the edge, he said.
They came.
He pushed them
and they flew...

Guillaume Apollinaire

Staying away from the edge, from our fears of defeat and loss, is what comfort zones are all about. Each of us lives in a box, its bottom, sides and top constructed from the assumptions and ideas of our society, our culture, our environment, our childhood and life experiences. These limiting beliefs form the walls of our "box"—a unique and personal construct, invisible to the eye, but very real in its impact on our lives.

Our comfort zone is supposed to help make life predictable, safe and secure. But as Andre Gide remarked about staying safe, "One doesn't discover new lands without consenting to leave shore for a very long time."

For many of us, however, our comfort zones become boring, so we make changes as a means of learning or doing something new, or simply to make life more interesting. The problem is, most of the changes we make are much like my friend's associate moving furniture around in his home: same furniture, slightly different location, a fresh look for a few days—but all within the same old box. At its worst, when we haven't made a genuine shift in our attitudes prior to making the change, this kind of rearranging—like getting a new job, or a new boyfriend or girlfriend—is like rearranging the deck chairs on the Titanic.

It doesn't matter which seat you sit in and where it is located, the ship (your life) is still going down.

Each of us often wants to get out of our box, but there is a problem: *The instructions for getting out of the box are written on the outside of the box.*

Getting out of the box of your limiting beliefs and creating new experiences and accomplishments means making a leap of faith. It means going for it before knowing for certain that you will reach your goal. And jumping into the unknown is not exactly what we human beings are good at. In fact, our fear of the unknown, of being out of control, looking foolish, or, at worst, dying—emotionally if not physically—is what we must confront when taking on any new challenge.

A bright and shining example of this phenomenon (our decidedly non-scientific name for it is "stuckness") is the tale of singer Barbra Streisand, who was terrified of performing live on stage. For 20 years she turned down lucrative concert offers that came her way. Like you and me in more mundane situations, her limiting beliefs were in the way. Finally, in 1995, she overcame her fears to give one of the most exciting concert performances ever seen.

It took her a long while to get there, to be able to acknowledge as she did: "I could either say, 'I am terribly frightened and fear is terrible and awful and it makes me uncomfortable, so I won't do that because it's uncomfortable,' or I could say, ' Get used to being uncomfortable. It is uncomfortable doing something that's risky. But so what? Do you want to stagnate and just be comfortable?'"

Streisand's limiting beliefs must have begun to feel like a millstone around her neck. It was not like she needed the money or the fame or more adoration from her millions of fans. Something inside was nagging at her; something was making her comfort zone feel very uncomfortable indeed, so uncomfortable that facing her fears became secondary to getting back on stage. The unfortunate thing is that there was no need for her return to have taken so long.

Barbra Streisand's decision, like many important life decisions, was made in a split second. The worrying about it took twenty years. There was no magic formula, simply a change in attitude from "What if I fail?" to "My dreams and goals are more important than my limiting beliefs and fears." Her image became less important than her need to be herself, express herself and perform.

And there was a stronger reason for her courageous decision to perform live. It was to raise money—big money— and publicity for a charity that is very dear to her, curing AIDS. She discovered there was something bigger and more important than her fears, something that could only be found in the act of giving. Giving her gift required that she move past her fears and sing live.

Be unreasonable

Getting free of your box involves the same sort of risk, but the true rewards that life has to offer are found nowhere else. Author Cecil Beaton, once said, "Be daring, be different, be impractical; be anything that will assert integrity of purpose and imaginative vision against the play-it-safers, the creatures of the commonplace, the slaves of the ordinary." I would add to that, be outrageous—if that is what it takes. And, above all, when society suggests you be reasonable, be the opposite. Be unreasonable. In that leap into the void, there are no short cuts and few soft landings. The rewards are a life that is full and rich and even extraordinary!

> "This is the true joy in life, the being used for a purpose recognized by yourself as a mighty one; the being thoroughly worn out before you are thrown on the scrap heap; the being a force of Nature, instead of a feverish, selfish little clod of ailments and grievances complaining that the world will not devote itself to making you happy."

George Bernard Shaw wrote that in the "epistle dedicatory" to his play *Man and Superman*. Elsewhere he wrote:

> "Life is no 'brief candle' to me; it is a sort of splendid torch which I have got hold of for the moment, and I want to make it burn as brightly as possible before handing it on to future generations."

Or in other words: Carpe Diem—seize the day! All the concepts about stepping out of your comfort zone mean nothing until you decide that your essential purpose, vision and goals are more important than any of your self-imposed limitations.

ORDINARY PEOPLE...

...believe that they are "not enough"

...often say they want to change as long as there's no risk or pain

EXTRAORDINARY PEOPLE...

..."clean up" and let go of any negative or self-limiting patterns from their past

...acknowledge their unique and extraordinary existence as human beings

...Carpe Diem—Seize the Day!

~ 12 ~

CHANGING GEARS:
LIFE'S BETTER WHEN YOU FIRST
SWITCH INTO NEUTRAL

*Whoever undertakes to set himself up as a judge
in the field of truth and knowledge is shipwrecked
by the laughter of the Gods.*

Albert Einstein

When you boil it down, life is made up of our minute-to-minute experiences. And once we begin to become more aware, at some point we discover a fundamental truth: life is not positive or negative, it just is.

The great Australian tennis player, Rod Laver, was once asked how he seemed to be able to win most of the time, even when he was on the brink of defeat. Laver said, "I keep going for my shots the same as always. I reckon the ball doesn't know what the score is." Right. The ball is neutral. It doesn't care. It does not feel any stress from a tight situation. Players do. What distinguishes the great players from the almost-great is a performance while under pressure.

Of course, life's events don't usually seem neutral. They seem good or bad, right or wrong, lucky or unlucky. Of course, that's because we don't usually perceive life as it is. Most of the time, each of us perceives the world through the filters of our own values, beliefs and experiences.

As I write this, I often pause to look out the window at these beautiful Rocky Mountains, and remember once again that everything I see is neither right nor wrong, good nor bad. It is totally neutral. How I choose to interpret what I see, how I judge my environment, governs my experience of this moment. In order to make this point about personal filters clear to students, I often ask two questions: "Have you ever been somewhere that was supposed to be fun, a party, for example, or Disneyland, and had a lousy time?" Just about everybody can honestly answer "yes" to this question.

Then, I ask: "Have you ever been somewhere or done something that is supposed to be boring or drudgery, like washing the dishes or going to work on a cold, wet day, and had a great time?" Invariably, most people answer "yes." I follow that by stating, "It is obviously not the activity or the event itself that brings happiness or sadness. It must be something about you."

Then I ask a volunteer from the group to come up front to help me demonstrate this point. I say to him or her: "Suppose you and I were at an outdoor party, out on the lawn, and you'd never met me before; suddenly I ran up to you and slapped you hard, like this, on the back." And I give the participant a hearty whack on the back. "What's your reaction?" I ask. "Anger!" is the usual response or "Surprise!" or "Who do you think you are, hitting me on the back?" To which I reply: "What if I say to you, 'Boy, I'm glad I killed that wasp before it stung you! Those wasps can sting like a gunshot wound!' Does your reaction change?" Invariably, the participant says: "Yes. Now I feel grateful, appreciative. I want to thank you."

The point is a simple one, yet so easy to overlook. It's not events that determine our moment-to-moment experience of life. It's how we interpret those events. In and of themselves, all events are neutral.

So to save you and I an e-mail exchange…yes, in your experience, the death of your parents was or will be a neutral event. In your experience, the latest terrorist bombing was a neutral event. In your experience your teenager's coming home late with alcohol on his or her breath was a neutral event. It's all interpretation. Of course, should my teenage daughters do it, IT'S AN EVENT! (That's a joke, folks.)

The choice called drama

The American talk show host Dr. Laura Schlessinger is, among other positive qualities, at times a bit too mean-spirited for your author. The good doctor does, when it is introduced by callers, handle "drama" in a really effective way. She simply refuses to entertain it, respond to it, answer questions about it or engage in it personally. It is one of her most positive qualities.

The payoffs for choosing drama as a way to handle the events of your life are myriad. How about temporarily satisfying, long, go-nowhere conversations that serve to lower the intelligence level of all involved? Or, how about an entertaining way to avoid looking at how the event was just the event —unless you are committed to not objectively describing it for some reason hidden away in your belief system? Or, how about having this neutral event be exaggerated so that your life appears more exciting than you actually experience it?

Drama is a way to avoid simply looking at "what is" while simultaneously engaging others in a dysfunctional pursuit. Get over it. It's all interpretation and drama only serves to take you further away from any positive resolution.

The choice called stress

How many times have you been running late for an appointment, only to find yourself stuck in traffic? It is frustrating and stressful. Right? Wrong. It's a traffic jam. It's neutral. It has no opinion. It is you who decides to make it an anxiety-ridden event or an enjoyable one. You have the choice. You can sit there in anger and frustration, or you can accept things as they are, switch on the radio, listen to some music—and relax. Getting wound up about it will change nothing, except to fill your day with stress.

I remember one day being in a long line at the bank, waiting my turn to conduct some urgent business with the teller. I noticed I had started being irritated and anxious at this delay in my oh-so-important life. Then I looked around at other people in the line. Some were obviously angry, one was whistling, a couple looked bored, one was moving in rhythm to the music from a Discman he was holding. It dawned on me yet again that, unconscious or not, we were each choosing the experience we were having at that moment. The line was neutral.

There is a huge difference in your life experience when you fight and resist life, versus when you are accept it as it is. Spending your life in anger and frustration because the world refuses to be how you think it should be creates constant stress and tension. Noticing your judgments, letting reality be what 'it is,' living in the real moment "that is" brings an experience of harmony and ease. How I feel only matters to me. The building doesn't care. The traffic doesn't care. The line at the bank doesn't care. A shift into neutral gets me off it, and allows me to experience well-being and contentment instead of rage and irritation.

A century before Christ, the Greek Stoic philosopher, Epictetus, noted: "Men are disturbed not by things that happen, but by their opinions of the things that happen."

Why give up a joyful, fulfilling experience of life to an outside event you can't control?

ORDINARY PEOPLE...

...allow circumstances to determine their experience of life

...enjoy drama and all the attention it brings them

...experience stress as distress

EXTRAORDINARY PEOPLE...

...see events as neutral–available for interpretation

...avoid drama and those who bring it to them

...choose their experience in every circumstance

~ 13 ~

ATTITUDE'S NO PLATITUDE

*Attitude, to me, is more important than the facts. It is more important than the past, than education, than money, than circumstances, than failures, than successes, than what other people may think or say or do. It is more important than appearance, giftedness or skill. It will make or break a company, a church, a home...
I am convinced that life is ten percent of what happens to me and ninety percent of how I react to it. And so it is with you.*

Charles Swindell

We humans have beliefs, attitudes, opinions and judgments about everything. Most of these beliefs we take for granted—so much so that we're not consciously aware of how they determine our experience. One of the keys to creating new possibilities in life is to understand how these pre-judgments, these filters, actually determine the outcomes we produce in our lives. Our attitudes, opinions, beliefs and judgments are, simply put, our attitudes, opinions, beliefs and judgments. They are not universal truths.

Our filters are the decisions we make about ourselves, other people and the world based on our experiences. Once in place, these filters instantly and automatically determine our reality. The phrase, "Seeing is believing," is often explained as, "I wouldn't have believed it if I hadn't seen it." In truth, our minds work in the reverse. A much more accurate description of human perception is: "I wouldn't have seen it if I hadn't believed it."

Our minds don't perceive "reality" the way a camera simply records what's in front of it. Our minds are selective. We perceive what we expect to perceive, what fits into already established categories in our consciousness. This is dramatically proved by the example of a number of people, blind from birth, who have suddenly recovered their sight as adults. Although they can "see," what they are able to perceive is a confusing, disconcerting jumble of shapes and colors. Their minds have never learned to "see." They have no categories to fit their perceptions into, no learned expectations—no filters, to use our term. As a result, the long dreamed of experience of regaining sight is terrifying and disorienting—and some people who regain their sight as adults end up voluntarily going back to living a blind person's life again.

How it works with all of us is that we "see" what matches our beliefs—what we believe to be right or true. What runs contrary to our beliefs we overlook, or explain away as an exception to the rule. Unfortunately, many of our beliefs limit us and keep us from truly "seeing" and living up to our full potential. The popular saying "seeing is believing" is actually dead wrong. To drive this idea home once again, the accurate expression would be "what we believe determines what we see."

What is "The Truth"?

Angela was in her late thirties, recently divorced, and had knockout good looks. I met her with friends for a party at her home, where tall bookshelves sagged under the weight of dozens of self-help books. I knew her as a successful professional and she'd attended one of our introductory events a few years before—and she was angry, really angry.

"Listen, Robert," she said, "I've read just about all there is to read on having my life work better. I've got a whole wall full of self-help books. All you know-it-all gurus and facilitators say how important it is to keep your agreements and be responsible, be honest and trusting, and all the rest of that garbage. Well, I do keep my agreements. I am responsible and I'm honest. But you know what? I'm just about the only one who lives that way. People let me down all the time. They're never honest, and rarely keep their agreements. So, I've decided to hell with them. People are not worth being with. Who needs them?"

Pretty strong stuff. I looked at her and smiled. "Boy, Angela," I said, "you seem pretty angry right now. Who are you so angry with?"

"My ex-husband, for one," she said, "for not standing by me. And my business partner who stole two hundred thousand dollars from me. And the lawyer who helped him get away with it. And my mother who told me that it's my fault my husband left me. As far as I'm concerned, they can all go to hell."

"I hear that you're angry at a lot of people you feel have lied to you and betrayed you, and even made you wrong for what you've suffered. You may be right about who's to blame; however, do you want to go on this way, feeling angry and betrayed? Do you want to go on suffering like this?"

"No, actually, I don't," she said. "I'd like to let go of all this negativity and get on with my life. I feel like I've been stuck in this same place for two years."

"I'm glad to hear that, Angela," I said. "But to get unstuck and get on with your life, you're going to have to give up something you've been hanging onto for a long time. Do you know what that is?"

She paused. "Blaming everybody else and being right about this?" she said, reinforcing my belief that most people actually already know what stops them in life.

"You took the words right out of my mouth," I said. "You are blaming everybody else for not living up to your rigorous standards. The universe has been trying to send you a wake-up call for years—and you haven't been listening. Your husband leaving you, your business partner cheating you—these aren't accidents happening to poor, innocent you. You've created them. You're an intelligent and powerful woman—powerful enough to push everybody away from you so you're now all alone against the world.

"Like the rest of us, Angela," I went on, "you've created a reality to match your beliefs. Unfortunately, it looks like those beliefs include 'You can't trust anyone,' and 'Nobody keeps their agreements or tells the truth'—except you. So you get to be right. But look at the prices you're paying. All this anger and negativity and recycling of old judgments."

"It's true," she said …and the tears started to flow right in the middle of her party.

"Do you want the really bad news?" I said. "In being so right, you're cutting yourself off from most of the world and seriously limiting your chances of finding a loving relationship. You're also giving away your power. Even worse, you're giving it to those people you say you can't trust to be honest or to keep their word. You are handing the authorship of your life to people you say you don't want to be around. You're allowing those people to run your life."

She sighed. "I don't know if I can give up blaming other people just like that," she said. "I've been doing it for a long time."

"Well," I said, "it's your life. You can go on in exactly the same way you've been living it, gathering evidence to support your belief that it's you against the world, that nobody can be trusted. You can find another business partner who'll let you down, and another husband who'll leave you, and keep on being right. Of course, don't expect anything to change. It won't. You'll recreate the same old pattern, over and over again. Is that what you want?"

"No, it's not," she said.

"Then, bottom line, you'll need to give up all the excuses that playing victim and blaming everybody else provide for you. You realize, don't you, that all this accusing others is just a way to avoid looking at yourself. As long as your business partner's to blame, or your husband, you never have to face yourself honestly and see your responsibility in creating what's happened."

"That's going to be painful to confront," she said.

"Not as painful as years of anger and bitterness and disappointment," I said. "Even if it is, even if it's more painful, once you face up honestly and stop running away from responsibility, you'll be through with it. The pain will be over.

"If you keep on playing victim, the pain will go on and on. There'll be no end to it. If you want things to change, you're going to need to risk."

A few days later, I sent Angela a fax with a quote from Helen Keller, the extraordinary woman who could neither hear nor see. She wrote in *Let Us Have Faith*:

> "Security is mostly a superstition. It does not exist in nature, nor do the children of men as a whole experience it. Avoiding danger is no safer in the long run than outright exposure. Life is either a daring adventure, or nothing. To keep our faces toward change and behave like free spirits in the presence of fate is strength undefeatable."

Bats, bugs and birds: a lesson in reality

If you are now beginning to see that our filters, judgments and beliefs lie between us and experiencing the world as it really is, then hold on a minute, it gets even more interesting.

In his book, *Change Your Mind, Change Your World*, Dr. Richard Gillett puts the perception versus reality question into a scientific perspective. Gillett asserts that we don't have just gray filters or rose-tinted glasses, but four screens or representations between us and reality: distortion of the senses, distortions of language, innate prejudices, and generalization from past experience. He further wrote:

"There is no such thing as seeing the world 'realistically,' because our very sense organs and brain mechanisms are highly selective ...For example, we can see wavelengths of light only between about 400 and 700 millionths of a millimeter. This is a tiny proportion within the vast band of electromagnetic waves...most electromagnetic information simply passes us by...other creatures with different coding systems see 'reality' differently. A goldfish can look through its bowl and see the infrared remote control beams that operate TVs and video players. If a goldfish took to burglary, it would have the advantage of being able to see infrared beam of an intruder alarm system.

"The housefly has a flicker fusion frequency of 300 per second, which means it can separate 300 different images per second. The human flicker fusion frequency is comparatively slow...In one sense, the fly on the wall has a more accurate picture of reality than we do. Reality is truly in the eye of the beholder."

Gillett goes on to compare the senses of humans to those of such diverse animals as crabs, spiders, bats, birds, insects and even elephants. When it comes to the perception of the real world, many other creatures "see" more of the reality of life than we do. On most scales of sensation, human beings are pretty far down the list of great "seers." But high up or low down, in the final analysis we are stuck—or maybe blessed—with our particular vantage point. Our perception, comparatively poor though it may be, remains the only reality we have.

Despite what science has to say about our rather limited perception, we nevertheless enjoy something other creatures do not: the ability to choose our attitude. And attitude, for human beings at least, is everything. Your attitude will not change you or your world. It will do something even greater.

Attitude will change the way you see yourself and your world—and perception, after all, *is* your world, even if a housefly does see it better.

ORDINARY PEOPLE...

...often fail to recognize how their own belief system creates their reality

...blame others, themselves, circumstances, and on and on

EXTRAORDINARY PEOPLE...

...acknowledge that they create their own experience, their perceptions

...choose attitudes that positively support and further their journey through life

~ Part 3 ~

Responsibility
Feeling great versus feeling lousy

~ 14 ~

TO CHOOSE OR NOT TO CHOOSE?

*Liberty, taking the word in its concrete sense,
consists in the ability to choose.*

Simone Weil

Does freedom of choice really exist? Are we really the authors of our own lives? Or is choice an illusion? Maybe we only seem to choose what to do and where to go. Maybe in reality our actions, our feelings, and even our thoughts are controlled by circumstances, one event leading to the next mechanically, like a line of dominos. Perhaps everything that happens has been predetermined, so that it was inevitable that you would be reading this sentence in this book at this precise moment of your life. Or maybe it's all your choice.

This question of free will has been debated by philosophers for centuries, and I have no desire to add to the sea of ink that has been spilled arguing for one intellectual stance or another. My perspective is that often intellectual understanding is the booby prize in the game called life. The intellectual understanding of something, while it may be interesting, doesn't change anything. It may be interesting to debate how many angels can dance on the head of a pin; however, in the real world, in practical terms, and whatever intellectually consistent, logically defensible answer we arrive at, whether right or wrong, *makes no difference in the matter of our lives.*

The issue of choice is the same. There are eloquent philosophical arguments for free will, and equally eloquent arguments for determinism. If I'm good at arguing, I may be able to convince you intellectually that human beings do have free will and choice—or that they don't. Either way, the intellectual answer by itself won't make any difference in how you live your life, in whether you experience joy or feel depressed and miserable. That's why it's the booby prize.

So, I'd like to approach the question of choice from a different perspective. Here's what I'd like you to ask yourself: Which way of approaching your life will maximize your feelings of personal power, autonomy, freedom, enthusiasm, and self worth? Living as though you have the power to choose what happens in your life? Or living as though you have no choice, as though you are just a pawn in someone else's game?

The above questions are not intended to foster an empty intellectual debate. How you answer these questions will have a powerful impact on your moment-to-moment experience of life—right now. If I operate as if I have choice, I automatically increase my sense of empowerment, of control over my own destiny, of integrity and self-esteem. If I operate as if I am a victim of circumstances, or destiny, or fate, or my genetic programming, I automatically increase my sense of weakness, helplessness, powerlessness, and of being out of control. The difference is immediate and tangible, in my experience of life and, most importantly, in my results. It's a fact that if I feel more powerful and in control, that my performance, my real-world results, will improve dramatically.

The experience of no choice, no options, no way to make a difference, is the experience of hopelessness and discouragement. My attitude about choice makes a crucial difference in whether I will create the experience of living an extraordinary life. I suggest strongly that it might be useful, simply useful, to adopt the attitude that we always can choose.

~ 15 ~

DO YOU REALLY HAVE TO?

*Practically all human misery and serious emotional
turmoil are quite unnecessary—not to mention
unethical. You, unethical? When you make yourself severely
anxious or depressed, you are clearly acting against you
and being unjust and unfair to yourself.*

Albert Ellis

If you're like most people, there are lots of things in your life that you do, maybe every day, that you think of as "have to's." I have to get up early. I have to leave my kids in a daycare center. I have to battle rush-hour traffic. I have to go to work. I have to sit in endless meetings. I have to do what my boss tells me to even when I know it's a mistake. I have to be polite to people I don't like. I have to clean the house. I have to discipline my children. I have to pay taxes. I have to live alone. I have to…I have to…I have to…

Think about it. Any time your attitude about something that you do is "I have to," what will your experience inevitably be? I suggest it will be negative. Inevitably. I have to go to work, and when I do, I feel _____ (fill in the blank—perhaps bored, pressured, overworked—all negative). I have to leave my kids in a daycare center, and when I do I feel _____ (perhaps fearful, guilty, frustrated, resigned—all negative). I have to pay taxes and when I do I feel _____ (probably angry, cheated, impoverished—more negativity). I have to work all day and then come home and cook dinner and clean the house and when I do I feel _____ (absolutely overwhelmed, exhausted, resentful—totally negative.)

So, every time I approach an activity in my life as a "have to," as something I have no choice about, I create a negative experience for myself. Since most of us spend the majority of our time doing things that we experience as "have to's" for us, most of our days are filled with negative experiences of one kind or another. If you doubt this statement, next time you're driving to work on a freeway or taking a bus or subway or an airline flight, take a look at the faces of the people commuting to work. How do most people look? Bored, tired, irritated, resigned—in a word, unhappy. Why? Because most people are saying to themselves: "I have to go to work" or "I have to commute" or "I have to travel for business."

Is it actually true, however, that there are lots of things in my life that I "have to" do—things that I have no choice about? On the surface, it certainly seems that way sometimes, doesn't it? However, is it really true?

Have to, choose to…what's the difference?

Let's do a simple exercise to explore at a deeper level whether in fact "I have to" is actually the truth about lots of the things that you do in your life.

Think of something among your daily activities that you say you "have to" do—something you don't want to do and feel forced or obligated to do—yet actually do on a fairly regular basis. I'll give you an example of how the exercise works, and you can follow along and do it for yourself.

Pick a "have to" from your life—a real one, something you do frequently. Let's say, for example, that you don't like your job, or your boss, and every morning you wake up and say to yourself: "Oh no, morning already. I have to get up and go to work." So, you would start the exercise by writing down:

    I HAVE TO GO TO WORK.

What I'm really communicating to myself when I say this, of course, is: "I have no choice. I hate going to work, I don't want to go to work, but I have to." No choice. Is this really true? Well, let's find out. I invite you to get a pencil and a piece of paper and write down a real, live "have to" from your life and do the exercise along with me.

The next step is to look at what will happen if you *don't* do what you say you have to do. Like this:

    IF I DON'T GO TO WORK, THEN _____.

What would the consequences be, in the real world? Probably something like this:

    IF I DON'T GO TO WORK, THEN I'LL LOSE MY JOB.

Do this step with the 'have to' that you're working with. Then follow along with me to the next step:

IF I LOSE MY JOB, THEN _____.

What would happen, in the real world? Most likely, something like this:

IF I LOSE MY JOB, THEN I WON'T HAVE ENOUGH MONEY TO PAY FOR THE THINGS I NEED.

Do this step with your "have to." Then continue along with me in the same format, until you get to the bottom line, like this:

IF I DON'T HAVE ENOUGH MONEY TO PAY FOR THE THINGS I NEED, THEN I"LL HAVE TO BORROW MONEY FROM MY FAMILY.

IF I BORROW MONEY FROM MY FAMILY, THEN I'LL FEEL LIKE A FAILURE.

IF I FEEL LIKE A FAILURE, THEN I'LL FEEL UNWORTHY.

IF I FEEL UNWORTHY, THEN I'LL FEEL DEPRESSED.

IF I FEEL DEPRESSED, THEN I'LL FEEL LIKE LIFE'S NOT WORTH LIVING.

Let's say that feeling like life's not worth living is the bottom line for you—that it doesn't get any worse than that.

THEREFORE…I CHOOSE TO WORK.

What does this exercise demonstrate? Well, notice that when you say, "I have to go to work," what you're saying to yourself is that you have no choice. But, in reality, do you have a choice? Yes, as the exercise clearly shows, you can choose not to go to work. Of course, if you choose not to go to work, you may have to deal with some negative consequences, including losing your job and not having any money—not to mention feelings of failure, unworthiness, depression, and perhaps even suicide. So, actually, going to work is not only your choice, it's the best choice you have in your current situation. If you had a better choice than going to work, obviously you'd take it. And you don't. Going to work is your choice, and it's the best choice you have.

Now, of course, you might say that going to work is nowhere near as good a choice as winning the lottery or inheriting a million dollars, so that you don't need to work. Yet those are fantasy choices, not real choices. They're not available. If they were real choices for you, obviously, you'd make them.

If you take the time to do this exercise with every one of the things in your life that are "have to's" for you, you'll discover that everything you do is your choice. And not only that, everything you do is actually the best choice that's available to you right now. Not the best choice among all the possible choices you can dream up, but the best choice among the actual choices you have at this time. This can be an incredibly liberating realization and practice.

Grunge is not just music and fashion

What kind of experience do I inevitably create for myself whenever I see something I do as a "have to"? A negative experience—"the grungies." Approaching anything I do as a "have to" automatically generates the grungies: everything from feeling angry, annoyed vengeful, irritated and indifferent, to sad, isolated, frustrated, revengeful, powerless and resigned. "I have to" is often where lifelessness, anxiety, depression and victimhood begin. There's a large part of the pharmaceutical industry dedicated to helping us medicate the grungies resulting from our "have to's" as a quick fix solution instead of our taking responsibility for our choices.

Given that your life is made up of your experiences moment-to-moment, having the attitude of "I have to" about anything you do condemns you to spend a lot of your time feeling lousy. If that is what you want, go right ahead (if you think you have to). And think about it: Did you ever feel joyful or excited by saying "I have to" about anything? Absolutely not. Joy and excitement in life come when I experience the actions I take as my choices.

Fine, so if you don't want to go on feeling grungy, what can you do? Simply this: Instead of thinking "I have to," start thinking "I choose to." Start saying "I choose to" to yourself about everything that you do. After all, it's your choice anyway, even if your choice is to operate from a position of "I have to." So why not just come out and express your real choices, and in so doing, experience your own power? Approaching everything you do as "my choice" will automatically create positive experiences in your life, as inevitably as "I have to" will create negative ones. You might not feel like going to work, but if you're going to go anyway, why not choose it instead of making it another "have to?" Holding the attitude of "I choose to" and building into a habit will help you enjoy your work…and your life. Start today. It works. Or would you rather choose the grungies?

~ 16 ~

FEEL GREAT OR GRUNGY—
THERE IS NO THIRD WAY

*Born under a bad sign, I been down since I
begin to crawl. If it wasn't for bad luck,
I wouldn't have no luck at all.*

"Born Under a Bad Sign"
Blues singer Albert King

So, what's the bottom line, in terms of real-world results and real-world experience of life, regarding freedom of choice? Well, you can dream up all sorts of imaginary scenarios, but there are actually only two ways to live your life:

1. As if you have little or no choice, so that you feel trapped by all the things that you "have to" do. And whenever anything goes wrong, you blame it on other people or your "bad luck" or something outside yourself. When you live this way, you inevitably end up experiencing life as a victim (more about this later).
2. As if everything is your choice, so that you determine what happens in your life, including your reactions to events, by the decisions you make. This is the foundation for living your life in a truly responsible way (more about this later, too).

You might think that there is some in-between stance, some middle way, between "I have no choice" and "Everything is my choice." I suggest that this is an illusion. I suggest that in the real world, you can live your life in one of two ways: You can live as a victim of circumstances or luck or your parents or your boss, your wife or husband, your children, or *something*. Or you can live responsibly, as if what happens in your life is a result of the choices *you* make, so that you are in charge of your life.

There is no in-between. It's one or the other. Take your pick—it's clearly your choice.

O.K... SO NOW YOU UNDERSTAND THAT EVERYTHING IN LIFE IS A CHOICE... RIGHT?
RIGHT!!!
GOOD. NOW DID I CHOOSE THIS TIE?
YES! ABSOLUTELY! OF COURSE! YES, LIFE IS A CHOICE!
DAMN RIGHT YOU DID!
YOU CHOSE IT MAN!
NONSENSE!!
? !! ? ?! ?
HEY, GET REAL. DO YOU REALLY BELIEVE I WOKE UP THIS MORNING AND THOUGHT: WOW, WHAT A FABULOUS SUNNY DAY, I THINK I'LL GET AN EXPENSIVE LENGTH OF SILK, TIE IT TIGHT AROUND MY NECK AND LEAVE IT THERE FOR TEN HOURS. I DIDN'T CHOOSE THIS TIE, SOCIETY DID, MY CULTURAL ENVIRONMENT DID. ALL I DID WAS SELECT THE DESIGN.
?? ???

Life's a choice (or maybe not...)

At this point, maybe you're saying: "OK, so I can see how things work better if I act as though everything in life is my choice. But what about 'The Truth?' I need to be certain! Is everything really my choice? Or am I just fooling myself?"

Before I attempt to answer that question once and for all, I'd like to tell you a story of a man who devoted the greater part of his adult life to traveling the world in search of meaning. He'd read all the great spiritual masters and philosophers, been involved in all the great religions and sought the counsel of every noteworthy writer and teacher.

He'd exhausted himself in his lifelong quest until, finally, after many months trying to arrange an audience with a highly regarded and secretive guru who lived atop a remote mountain in the Himalayas, he arrived battered and bruised at the guru's mountain top retreat. Kneeling in front of the great master, he asked, "Please, guru, what is the meaning of life?" The loin-clothed hermit looked with great wisdom down his long, wispy beard. Minutes passed. Then, gazing serenely into the man's eyes, he spoke. "Life," he said softly, "is a river."

The man looked stunned. "Listen," he said angrily, "I've spent my entire life in search of meaning, and I come all the way up here for you to tell me life is a river?!" Clearly taken aback, the guru said nervously, "Well, err...maybe it's not."

I've said that life works when you and I operate as if everything in life is our choice, right? Which means that, for all practical purposes, I'm telling you that everything in life is your choice. Well, err...maybe not. Maybe God is up in the heavens somewhere laughing at Her cosmic joke because She knows that your entire life is preordained, that She has planned everything—every breath, every action, every thought, every moment—for you in advance, allowing you the illusion that you are choosing. I don't know.

What I do know for certain, what I can guarantee you is, illusion or not, operating as the chooser—and therefore the author of your life—gives you the experience of empowerment. And with the experience of personal power, you will be able to accomplish more of what you want. Interestingly, you will find that you will also create space for the people around you—your loved ones and friends—to better experience their own power.

Be clear: What I am talking about here is not some "Truth" (note the capital T). Experiencing ourselves "at choice" is about having our lives work better, about a richer, deeper and more fulfilling life, about getting off the victim treadmill and living an extraordinary life.

Hate the "grungies"? No, we love 'em!

People are not stupid. I say this again and again because the ways in which we sometimes act against our own best interests can often appear to be very stupid indeed. In the last section, I said that the human tendency to compare what we've actually got with an idealized fantasy choice is one of the sources of all the "have to's" in our lives. The other source, of course, is the hidden benefits—the payoffs—that we get when we turn "I choose to" into "I have to." These payoffs are so powerful and so seductive, in fact, that we're willing to put up with all the grungy feelings that "I have to" produces. You could say we are most happy being miserable.

Here's an example: Let's say I agree to go on a week-long whitewater rafting trip with you down the Grand Canyon, and at the last minute I call and tell you: "I'm really sorry, but I can't go. My boss won't give me the time off. I have to work that week."

What will my grungy feelings be? I'll feel disappointed that I'm not getting to go on vacation. I'll feel guilty and angry at myself for letting you down and backing out on you at the last minute. I'll feel depressed that I turned down the chance for an adventure. I'll feel resentful towards my boss for "making me" work, resentful of my job, overworked and under pressure—and maybe lots more. All kinds of grungy feelings are available here.

Additionally, will there be some payoffs, some hidden benefits? Absolutely. First of all, I don't have to risk those huge waves, which attract me but also truly frighten me. I don't have to admit to myself and to you that I'm afraid, which would make me look bad in your eyes and feel inferior in my own eyes. I can protect my image—and my own belief—that I am an outdoorsy, adventurous person with a passion for the thrills of whitewater rafting, while staying at home where it's nice and safe. I can reassure myself that I'm a valuable and much-needed employee, somebody really important to my boss and the company, which will make me feel superior.

I will probably do all of this unconsciously, without even being aware of it, and then wonder why my life seems dull and boring and limited, why I keep dreaming about adventure and excitement yet never seem to escape my safe daily routine.

~ 17 ~

SITTING ON THE FENCE IS A CHOICE, TOO

Pain is inevitable. Suffering is optional.

M. Kathleen Casey
How to Heal Depression

A stack of popular books exist which suggest that you and I are responsible for our feelings, that we have the freedom to choose our feelings, like choosing a tie in a department store.

This is, of course, a tremendous oversimplification. For most of us, it's true that we can sometimes stop and consciously choose our emotions. Have you ever been driving on a freeway, had someone cut in front of you dangerously close, and said to yourself: "OK, shall I get angry at this guy, or shall I let it go?" At times like this, there might be enough space between an event and our reaction that we can choose what we're going to feel.

Many times, it seems like we can no more choose our feelings than we can choose to be born. Something happens, and we react, instantly, automatically. However, even in these situations, we still have choice. *After* we experience our feelings, we have the freedom to decide how we will express them. It's a different kind of choice than choosing our emotions, but it is equally empowering and useful.

For example, if your boss promotes someone you think is incompetent to a position above you—and you think you should have been appointed instead—you might feel resentful and angry, especially if your belief is "I never get what I deserve!" Or you might feel sad and resigned if your belief is "A loser like me deserves to be overlooked." Whatever your feelings, once you notice your emotions, you have a choice. You can seethe with anger—or mope around in resignation—and let it affect your work and life to the point where you hate going to work every day. Or you can choose to let it go and win the emotional control game with your reactive self. Sounds simple, you say; however, when I get angry or sad, it's not that easy to just "let it go." How am I supposed to do that?

How not to wreck your day...and your life

Here are some insights that you may find helpful. To feel anger or sadness in response to an event may seem like a "natural" reaction. Remember what we learned earlier in this book: the events in our lives are not intrinsically good or bad, right or wrong, upsetting or pleasant. They're neutral. It's our interpretation of the event that creates our experience. Conditioned as we are by society growing up, we have come to think that it is inevitable to feel anger or sadness or jealousy or guilt in certain situations, because everyone agrees it is expected and "natural."

One key to letting go of your anger or sadness—or any negative emotion—is to own it as your feeling. It's not really what the boss did that's making you upset, it's the filters through which you're viewing the event. Once it has happened, it's your problem, not your boss's. Seeing what it is in you that's at the bottom of your angry or depressed or sad reaction will go a long way towards helping you let it go.

Another key to letting go of feelings is to understand their purpose. We hold on to anger because we believe (there's that word again) that by being angry we are "getting back" at the people we blame for our being upset. Or that if we stay angry enough, we can control people and get them to do what we want them to do. And we get sad so we can feel sorry for ourselves and get sympathy from others. Or, again, we can manipulate other people and get our own way. I know this may sound like a harsh judgment...and, look at your own pattern honestly and you may see some truth here.

Most importantly, most of the time, it doesn't work. The other people in your little drama don't care that you're upset. All we're doing is spoiling our own experience of life. There are a number of answers to your job problem. You might want to get it out into the open with your boss and clear it up, or look around for a new position where you are better appreciated. There is, however, only one answer to your anger or depression: Realize that negative emotions will only serve to wreck your day, or even the rest of your life. They will not affect your boss's day—remember, he or she, even if there is some awareness of your drama, probably doesn't care.

Imagine that your travel agent booked you a flight for an important business meeting and gave you the wrong departure time. You arrive at the airport proud of yourself thinking that you're really early and discover you're actually ten minutes too late…and you miss the flight. So, you are…angry, right? It's "natural." Yet the event itself has no anger attached to it, it's neutral. If you immediately get angry, it's not because that's the inevitable response. You've simply chosen anger (probably unconsciously) over the other available options.

Another person in the same situation, with a different set of filters, might interpret the situation as funny and laugh it off. Someone else might see it as just an unfortunate miscommunication, no big deal. Still others would be glad they missed the flight, because it gives them an opportunity to be better prepared for that important meeting while they await the next flight.

A correspondent friend of mine who travels constantly all over the world once told me that whenever he missed a flight or a flight was canceled, he always became alert to the opportunities that resulted. In fact, he said that, looking back, some of the most interesting people he'd met, and some of the most valuable experiences he'd had, were the result of a breakdown in the normal routine, such as missed transportation. Had he chosen anger and frustration at those times, he could not possibly have become alert to the opportunities the breakdown in normality presented. In any case, there was nothing to be gained, and a lot to be lost, by choosing anger and frustration.

Guilt is another emotion that people often feel is "natural." For example, suppose you're a mom with two young children and would like to stay home and be with them. However, so your family can have more money—and also because you get bored staying home with two little kids all the time—you go to work.

As a result, you can't be home with your children except at night and during weekends. And sometimes, they cry and say, "Mommy, stay home today," when you need to go to work.

"Naturally" you'll feel guilty, right? Well, not necessarily. Could you not feel guilty? Sure you could. In fact, you could feel good about providing the money to create a good environment in which your children may learn and grow while modeling a potentially positive life choice to them. You could feel proud of yourself for managing both a job and a family. Of course, when your children ask you to stay home and you choose to go to work, you could tell them how sorry you are, but what's the point of that? Being "sorry" is just an excuse to keep on working, while pretending to yourself (and your children) that you'd really rather stay home. Using the word "sorry" in this way is either an excuse to do it again or an avoidance of owning your choices.

Why sorry is silly

Saying "I'm sorry" in this way is a pretty widespread human phenomenon, about as widespread as feeling angry or guilty. On the surface, saying "I'm sorry" appears to communicate two things. First, it seems to be a way of asking for your forgiveness, on the grounds that "I didn't really mean to do what I did." And second, saying "I'm sorry" appears to promise or at least imply that "I won't do whatever I did in the future—it won't happen again. "Pretty innocent stuff, right?

Wrong again. If you're willing to look deeper, you'll see that "I'm sorry" is actually a very subtle and sneaky form of manipulation, both of other people, and of myself. A classic example is the man who on Friday night takes his week's pay and goes to the tavern and spends a bunch of it on getting rip-roaring drunk. When he wakes up in bed the next morning (with no memory of how he got there), of course the first thing he says to his wife is, "Honey, I'm sorry." What's the underlying message he's communicating? "I'm not responsible. I didn't really mean to get drunk – the devil made me do it. Don't blame me, it's not my fault."

The self-manipulation in "I'm sorry" can be even more subtle. Let's say I promise my son that I'll leave work early and come to his soccer game on Thursday afternoon. Then on Thursday afternoon I get caught in an important meeting and decide it would be embarrassing to get up and walk out before the meetings over—so I miss my little boy's soccer game. When I say "I'm sorry," it's not only a manipulation of my son, it's also a manipulation of myself. What kind of a "dad identity" do I want to claim? Perhaps a caring dad who can be counted on to keep his word, a role model for honesty and integrity?

What don't I want to admit to myself? That my son can't count on me – that I don't always tell the truth. That, in fact, I'm not a role model for honesty and integrity, even though I may preach about these things to my son. My identity to my colleagues is actually more important.

And what's the practical result of saying "I'm sorry" in this way? It gives me permission to repeat what I feel sorry about over and over again. If I let myself off the hook, and it wasn't really my fault, and I feel "sad," then I can do the same thing again tomorrow. And, of course, tomorrow I'll be "sorry" all over again. If my sorrow was authentic, there would be no repetition of the false, inappropriate behavior; yet most of the time, it is not authentic.

It's clear that saying "I'm sorry" in such a way, carries with it a full load of what psychologists call "secondary gain," a fancy term for a disguised benefit. These secondary gains can also be labeled "payoffs." When I feel "sorry" for something I did—or didn't do—for weeks or months or even years, then I'm experiencing guilt, and guilt, contrary to popular opinion, is laden with potential payoffs:

- It's a great way to get people to pity you and give you sympathy.
- It allows you to punish yourself for what you did. If you feel guilty enough, and suffer deeply enough, you will somehow have paid the price and be pardoned.
- It lets you to say to yourself, "I'm a good person, otherwise I wouldn't feel guilty. Only a bad person would do what I did and not feel guilty."
- It is safer to feel guilty and remain in the past than to take the risk of fully telling the truth to yourself, letting it go and then being confronted with the need to learn and grow from the experience.

Which of these payoffs might be your motive for choosing to feel guilty? Yes, I said choosing. Unconsciously, perhaps, and choosing, nonetheless.

I keep repeating that people are not stupid, and we're not. For every destructive emotion and limiting belief we hang onto, there are payoffs, hidden benefits. Why else would we hold onto them?

The next time you find yourself about to say "I'm sorry," do a gut check. Is this an authentic expression of regret and apology? Or, is it a way to avoid taking full responsibility for your choices? When you simply share your actual choices with the people in your life, beyond some initial discomfort, you'll be amazed at the improvement you create in your relationships. And, you'll be on your way to living a more authentic, more satisfying life, free of self-blame, guilt and regret.

Ordinary People…

…deny free will and choice as primary determinates in their lives

…have a belief and live from the perspective that circumstances rule their lives

…believe that something or someone else is the author of their life story

…are run by their feelings

…are often "sorry"

Extraordinary People…

…choose to live as if they chose the events, the circumstances of their lives

…include in their choices the choice to live an extraordinary life

…choose to author and direct their own life

…fully experience their feelings and resist the impulse to have their feelings control their choices

…are seldom "sorry;" they tell the truth about their behavior and their own choices

~ 18 ~

RESPONSIBILITY: DO YOU FEEL LIKE A SNOWFLAKE IN AN AVALANCHE?

Take your life in your own hands and what happens?
A terrible thing: no one to blame.
Erica Jong

First, a few words on the meaning of the word: "Responsibility" comes from the Latin *re spondere*, meaning "to promise something in return for something else," or "to answer for." In other words, if I am "responsible," I have the ability to answer for my actions. In and of itself, "responsibility" is neither positive nor negative. The word itself does not imply either praise for good deeds or blame for misdeeds. "Responsibility" is neutral.

Given the all-too-human tendency to look for excuses when we screw up—to find somebody or something to blame for our mistakes—it's no wonder that "responsibility" is all too often a synonym for "blame." In our everyday conversations, when we say that someone is "responsible," it is frequently another way of saying that we blame them. And when I say, "I'm responsible," what I often mean is that I blame myself and feel guilty or shamed.

Yet "responsibility" and "blame" are not synonymous. "Responsibility" is simply the capacity of adult human beings to give an honest account of their actions. And my Random House Dictionary of the English Language defines "account" as: "a verbal or written description of particular transactions or events." No praise or blame here, no right or wrong, good or bad. Just the facts.

As I've said, given our tendency to try to save face, to look good at all costs, simply accounting for our actions, without praise or blame, turns out to be no easy matter for most of us. This is especially true when something happens that hurts us, and we're looking around in anger to find someone to blame. In fact, when I suggest to people that they'd be much better off giving up blaming others (as well as themselves) and adopting a responsible point of view towards all the events in their lives, I often meet with strong opposition, even outrage. Whatever the identity we so carefully, and usually unconsciously, construct, we tend to defend it tenaciously.

It's not my fault

In one of our Extraordinary Living Seminars a bright young doctor (I'll call him Paul) communicated very directly that he thought my ideas about responsibility were wrong, if not downright dangerous. I had just asserted to the group that—no matter what happens in our lives—there is always value in looking at events from the responsible point of view.

Paul's hand shot into the air. "I'd like to challenge that," he said.

"OK," I said. "Stand up and tell us about something that happened to you that you had nothing to do with, where you were an innocent victim."

"No problem," he said. "Yesterday I was leaving the hospital, and when I came out of the elevator, the floor was all wet from just being mopped, and I slipped and twisted my right ankle. Badly. It really hurt. They have warning signs they're supposed to put out when they mop the floor, but there was no warning sign."

"And when that happened, sounds like you felt like a victim," I said.

"No kidding," he said. "But that wasn't the worst part. I limped out to my car, and as I was pulling out of the parking lot, some guy came barreling up the street and sideswiped the left side of my new BMW. It's going to cost over two thousand dollars to fix, and this guy doesn't have insurance. So my insurance is going to have to pay, which they told me is going to raise my premiums."

"That's a great victim story, Paul," I said. "And as a result of feeling victimized by the guy who mopped the floor, and then by the one who sideswiped your car, what have you been experiencing? Right now, as you tell the story, what are your feelings?"

"I feel pissed off at both of them," he said. "I feel that it's unfair. I feel ripped off, cheated, by the insurance situation. I feel like I don't deserve to have this happen to me."

"Right," I said. "You experienced the grungies. Any time you or I see ourselves as victims in any situation, that's what we get—a negative experience of some kind. As I've been saying, it's automatic."

"Don't you think most people here would feel the same way if it happened to them?" he asked.

"Maybe," I said. "But only because most people, like you, come at life as victims. When things like this happen, we look around for someone to blame. Or maybe we blame ourselves. So we have all these negative feelings we carry around. Let me ask you, Paul: Are you willing to look at these events you told us about from a different point of view?"

"OK," he said. "Why not?"

"Good," I said. "You just told us one version of what happened, from the victim point of view. Now let's look at these same events from the responsible point of view. Let's take the part about slipping on the wet floor and spraining your ankle first. If you look back at what happened, what choices did you make—what did you do or not do—so that you influenced things turning out exactly the way they did?"

Paul looked up at the ceiling and thought about this question. Finally, he said, "Well, now that I think about it, I was rushing. I was late leaving to pick up my girlfriend, and I was worried about her being mad at me, because I've been late a bunch of other times. To tell the truth, I didn't even look at the floor when I came out of the elevator."

"So, how you set yourself up to slip and sprain your ankle," I said, "was by not leaving on time, hurrying to get out to your car, and being distracted worrying about your girlfriend so that you didn't pay attention to things—like a wet floor."

"I guess so," he said.

"And how about getting your car sideswiped by the guy with no insurance. How'd you set that up?"

Paul smiled. "You can probably already see this coming," he said. "I was in a hurry and since my ankle was sprained, it was painful to use my right foot, so I didn't put on the brakes coming out of the hospital parking lot. I saw this guy coming, but I didn't stop. I thought I could beat him. But he was going faster than I thought, and because my ankle hurt, I couldn't hit the gas as hard as I usually would. So he smacked me."

"Paul," I said, "I want you to notice your experience right now. As you tell your story from the responsible point of view, how are you feeling?"

"I'm feeling relieved," he said. "The whole thing actually seems kind of funny right now." He paused and checked in with himself. "I'm definitely less angry at whoever mopped the floor and the guy who hit me. And less upset about feeling like it was unfair. I feel better."

"Exactly," I said. "When you're willing to look at things from the responsible point of view, your experience shifts from negative to positive. You get rid of the grungies. And you can let go of what's happened in the past and move on."

It's never too late to have a happy childhood

OK, fine, you get it, right? Well, maybe. Perhaps you're asking yourself: "What if I were just three years old when I my parents got a divorce and I was sent to live with my grandmother? And what if I were eight when I began to be sexually abused by my uncle? Or five when my father died? What happens to responsibility then? Surely, innocent children cannot accept responsibility for the sins of adults?

Good question, and remember, it's not events that make you a victim, nor do events make you responsible. It's how you interpret events that determine whether you're a victim or you're responsible, and that's your choice. It's entirely up to you. You can choose to be responsible and feel in charge and empowered, or you can allow yourself to be a victim of the past and experience all the grungy feelings that automatically come with victimhood.

To make this clearer, let me tell you about a man (I'll call him Joe) who said to the group:

"I'm sure you noticed that I have a withered leg," Joe said. "I had polio when I was a kid. In 1950, before they had the vaccine, I spent most of a year in a hospital. I could never play baseball or football in high school or go to a dance. I don't see how taking the responsible point of view can change all that."

"Thank you for your honesty, Joe," I said. "By way of an answer, let me tell you a story…

A tale of responsibility from a Nazi death camp

"In a seminar some years back, Joe," I said, "we were in the middle of a heated discussion about responsibility, just as we are now, when a young guy jumped up to tell me about an elderly man in his small group. In the 1940's, this man's entire family had been killed in Nazi concentration camps, and he was the only survivor. How in God's name, the young guy wanted to know, could I say that this man was anything except a victim? How could I say he was responsible for that experience?

"Before he could finish, the elderly gentleman referred to rose to his feet and asked the younger man to sit down, saying that he could speak for himself. I guessed that he was in his seventies, and as he began to speak his face filled with emotion and his hands began to tremble.

"'Robert,' he said, 'my young friend here has told you what happened to me and my family in the war. Like most everyone else here, he is unable to see how or why I should choose to look at what happened to me and my family from the responsible point of view. It is true that, like so many people of my era, I've considered myself the innocent victim of a brutal war for these last 40 years. Before today, I had never even thought about it in terms of responsibility. Certainly I am unable to forget those evil times and the horrors I suffered. But as for taking responsibility…I think I now see what you mean.

"'It seems I have taken responsibility without realizing it. At some point, I saw clearly that I had a critical choice to make. I could either live in terrible anger and resentment, as a victim, and ruin totally the rest of the life I've been blessed with. Or I could move forward and make the most of it. I chose to release the past, to move on. When I made that choice, I found that I could even start to forgive, and that freed me further. I guess, by your definition, Robert, I chose to take responsibility for what happened to me, for my mental health and for my well-being. Shouldn't that be the first priority for everyone? Beyond that, I try to do all I can to promote peaceful existence between people so that no such evils are allowed to happen again. Yes, I have chosen to be responsible and it's mostly because it allows me to live my life, today, more fully and be more available to the people I love. Thank you.'

"As he sat down there was first a stunned silence, and then loud applause as everyone stood, most, including me, in tears.

"I tell you this story, Joe," I said, "because what happened to you is in a way like what happened to the man in the concentration camp. He lost his whole family in the Holocaust. You suffered from polio as a child. In both cases, it was terrible and painful, more than anybody else will ever know. And it happened. You can't go back and change that, no matter how much you wish you could. You do, however, have a choice about how you approach that event, Joe, about the attitude you take towards it, right here, right now, even though it happened years ago."

Joe slowly nodded his head, so I kept going.

"From what you shared, it sounds like for years, right up until today, you've been feeling like a victim of polio, seeing what happened to you through a victim's eyes. That's a normal reaction, and I'm sure a lot of people in your life have supported you in seeing yourself as a poor, unfortunate victim of this admittedly terrible disease."

"You're right," he said. "My mother did it for years, and my wife does it now."

"It doesn't have to be that way, Joe," I said. "You don't have to go on feeling like a victim. Like the man in the story, you can choose to shift your attitude about what happened to you from victim to responsible. Not responsible meaning 'I'm to blame,' but responsible meaning 'I accept my polio as simply part of my life, something that happened. I can stop fighting it, stop wishing it hadn't happened, stop trying to change it. I give up my anger and my bitterness. I give up being a victim of polio. And I forgive myself. I give up my anger at me.'"

"I'm pretty sick of feeling like a victim," he said. "I'm ready to be responsible."

"I can see that you are," I said. "And if you're willing to make that choice, you'll find out what I discovered when I did this seminar—that it's never too late to start experiencing freedom and aliveness, no matter what happened in the past."

Responsibility: the balm of forgiveness

You might well think that only a saint could possibly forgive the horrors of something so horrendous and evil as a Nazi death camp. For most of us, forgiveness like that seems difficult, if not impossible. However, whether the event that happened to us is major or minor (by some external standard), as long as we feel victimized, we can never reclaim our personal power. Until we are willing to forgive, our power is given away to whomever or whatever victimized us.

So let's clear up a widespread misunderstanding of what forgiveness is all about. Many of us hang onto our anger and bitterness because we imagine that somehow we're continuing to punish the people who victimized us. We refuse to forgive, because that would be letting those people off the hook, and we want them to go on suffering, as we have. That's usually the primary "payoff" we're looking for in continuing to hate and resent.

In reality, however, our hatred and resentment have little or no effect on anybody, except ourselves. When I hate someone for what they did and refuse to forgive, the one who suffers is *me*. The idea that I'm causing somebody else to suffer by being angry at them is almost always an illusion, a fantasy. However, my own pain is very real.

The fact of the matter is that time alone does not heal all wounds. It's true that the initial pain loses its sharpness and becomes a dull, throbbing ache, still this ache doesn't just go away by itself. Only by taking responsibility for our own experience and actively forgiving (choosing to have a different kind of relationship with painful events from the past) can we heal and move on fully.

It's important to remember that forgiveness applies not only to our relationships with others, but with our relationship with our "self." If you're like most people, you have an easier time forgiving others than you do forgiving yourself. Most of us beat up on ourselves much more than we beat up on others. And our motive is the same: to even the score. By punishing ourselves, we imagine that we can make ourselves pay for the mistakes we've made—and then everything will be OK. It doesn't work. With no self-forgiveness, the guilt and shame we feel only intensify, and we spiral downward, perhaps even thrashing ourselves into a state of intense emotional distress.

It is immensely valuable to ask yourself: "What's my payoff here? What do I get out of feeling guilt and shame and beating up on myself?"

Misery for a mountain man

A good example of this phenomenon is a professional mountain climber I know, whom I'll call Martin. Martin was in a horrifying disaster during a high altitude expedition, and a number of climbers died. Martin was lucky. He survived, wrote of his experiences and made a considerable amount of money from the book and television specials it spawned. Although he'd tried to rescue other climbers, he felt guilty and ashamed that he survived, that he didn't do more to help. His guilt got worse when he started making money out of the "tragedy." Eventually, his self-flagellation led to a serious depression.

"What could possibly be his payoff in all that misery?" you may be asking yourself. Well, by wallowing in self-pity and thrashing himself emotionally on a daily basis, he did get some friends to feel sorry for him and give him sympathy and attention. His really big payoff was that he could continue to think of himself as a man of courage and integrity, while behaving in exactly the opposite way. Martin had always thought of himself above all as a man who would risk his life to save other climbers who were in trouble. But when the moment came to take that risk, he hesitated, paralyzed by fear.

On top of this, Martin had always despised journalists who made their living writing about the misfortunes of other people. He thought of them as vultures. When the opportunity came, he found out that he was one of those vultures himself. His guilt and self-punishing were thus his way of not facing the truth about himself. Beating up on himself allowed Martin to maintain his idealized image of himself. After all, only a man of courage and integrity would feel bad about acting like a coward and a vulture.

I know Martin's story because he told it in one of our seminars, where he shared about how his guilt was crippling his life. By facing himself honestly, he realized that feeling guilty was his unconscious way of rationalizing to himself what he'd done, and ultimately, of giving himself permission to repeat the pattern again. The only way out of this trap, he saw, was to forgive himself for the past, and then start having the discipline to make sure that his future actions lined up with his principles.

My personal experience and noticing the experience of the hundreds of thousands of people I've worked with over the years tells me this about guilt: Guilt is produced by holding a standard for yourself and simultaneously violating that standard. You have limited choices to deal with guilt and eliminate the corrosive effect it has on your aliveness, relationships and results:

1. Don't do any action that doesn't meet your standards, that violates your values. Of course, almost always our awareness of guilt arrives after the action takes place so this choice is almost never available to us.

2. Lower your standards. Yes, I'm serious about this. Recognize that you actually are the kind of person that would do whatever it was that you did, and that holding on to a false sense of who you really are is ultimately self-defeating.

3. Take full responsibility for your action...learn what you need to learn...and let it go, leave it in the past where it belongs.

The many "Twelve Step" programs to heal additions include as one of the steps "making amends" and this effort to express full responsibility and "clean up" damage done to relationships seems to be very valuable to many people. You might want to consider it as another useful tool.

What the opposite of "responsible" looks like

I know a similar story which demonstrates the exact opposite of the powerful example of responsibility from the man who survived the concentration camp. This story is also from World War Two. I first heard it on a television news show in 1998.

A group of former British POWs were held in virtual slavery by the Japanese. They were brutalized so badly over a period of more than three years that most of their number died. Some of the survivors had been trying in vain for over 50 years to get an official apology and compensation from the Japanese government. Finally, in 1998, their case came to court in Tokyo before a three-judge panel. Their case was dismissed—with no apology and not even token compensation—in less than 20 seconds.

The news clip I saw was of the leader of their group, a 74-year-old Englishman, spitting on the steps of the Japanese parliament building and shouting angrily at the surrounding television cameras, "There is no justice in this country!" I lived in Japan for a significant number of my adult years and know the many cultural barriers that would need to be surmounted for Japan—as a nation or for an individual—to get through their resistance to addressing what they experience as shame, take responsibility for their actions and put that tragic period in their individual and collective pasts. I felt great compassion for the man, and something else as well.

A few months later I saw him being interviewed on the BBC television program, "Hardtalk," where for 30 minutes he vented his anger and frustration. It was a deeply saddening experience for me, not only because of all the atrocities he and his fellows had suffered, but because this essentially good man had lived his life in reaction to a tragedy. He had chosen to burden himself by carrying the pain and torment of his incarceration for more than half a century. He had wasted his life, to say nothing of the damage his bitterness and anger surely did to his family and friends.

What was this man's payoff, you might ask, for all these years of hatred, resentment and feeling victimized? Clearly, he had the illusion that somehow, by not forgiving, by not letting go of his anger, he was punishing the Japanese for what they did. And at the same time, he could hang onto a feeling of superiority, of somehow triumphing over his enemies. What was the price for these "secondary gains?" Fifty years of suffering, personally and for his family and everyone else in his life.

If you are not really at peace with what has happened in your life, then you have not truly accepted responsibility for the events themselves, and for your response to them. Any lingering resentment or regret simply means that you still want to lay blame, either at your own door or someone else's.

Like the man who suffered so greatly in the death camps, it would have been difficult for the British POW to simply forget what had occurred. Yet even though he couldn't forget, he could nevertheless choose to forgive, and thereby free himself from the past so he could get on with his life again. Clearly, the payoffs he received through all of those years from his self-cast role as martyr were more important to him than any sort of peace or happiness.

It reminds me of the story from the Zen tradition of the two monks walking beside a swift-flowing river.

The monks met a lovely young lady who wanted to cross the stream. She asked if one of the monks would carry her across. Having taken strict vows which did not allow them to touch women, the monks apologized and said they could not help her. After much pleading that her grandfather who lived on the other side was very ill and needed her help, one of the monks, much to the disapproval of the other, finally relented and carried the young woman across. The two monks continued on their way, the disapproving monk clearly steaming at what had happened remained silent. Eventually, he couldn't take it any more and asked angrily, "Why did you carry that woman across the stream when you know it is against our religious vows?" The second monk replied, "I only carried her across the stream. You've been carrying her all day."

My friend and founder of the Atlanta Consulting Group, Dr. Hyler Bracey, lives with disfiguring burns from a stock car driving accident. He's incredibly successful and has made a huge contribution to many people's lives including co-authoring the wonderful book *Managing from the Heart*. His latest career flies in the face of those who would say that he should use his disfigurement as an excuse to hide from others: he's sharing his love of old ship whistles and horns through appearing in parades—including the giant Macy's Thanksgiving Day parade in New York City—as an outrageously dressed maestro of Big Toot, his custom-made display and entertainment vehicle.

Perhaps you've heard or heard of the amazing public speaker W. Mitchell, a paraplegic also disfigured by burns. Mitchell inspires me with just his presence. Quoting from his website, "Having overcome two life-threatening and life-changing accidents—the first a fiery motorcycle accident and the second an airplane crash—Mitchell says: 'Before I was paralyzed there were 10,000 things I could do. Now there are 9,000. I can either dwell on the 1,000 I've lost or focus on the 9,000 I have left.'"

The unifying quality of these men, and of Helen Keller and Christopher Reeves and so many others, is how they've chosen to take responsibility for their lives and done so much to contribute to others, perhaps not in spite of their afflictions, even because of what happened to them.

Responsibility: the foundation of personal power

Let's summarize what we've been saying about responsibility. Responsibility is not the Truth with a capital T. It's a point of view that I can choose to take regarding all of the events in my life. If I choose to approach life from the responsible point of view, it means giving up my excuses, my avoidances, all the manipulative games I play when I feel like a victim. In return, what I gain is freedom, clarity and the empowering experience of being in control and in charge of my life.

Responsibility means seeing and acknowledging that my actions in every situation were crucial for it to turn out the way it did. And once an event has occurred, responsibility means accepting that event as part of my life, something to learn and grow from, without blaming others or myself. Viktor Frankl, the innovative psychiatrist who was a survivor of the Nazi nightmare wrote:

> "Man is ultimately self-determining. What he becomes—within the limits of endowment and environment—he has made out of himself. In the concentration camps…we watched and witnessed some of our comrades behave like swine while others behaved like saints. Man has both potentialities within himself; which one is actualized depends on decisions but not on conditions."

Naturally, in any situation, input from others and external events influence the shape of my life. Yet from the responsible point of view, my own input and attitude are the critical factors in determining the way things turn out. Everyone and everything contributes a stone or two to the arch, but my behavior is the keystone that holds the whole structure together. The act that releases me to freedom is recognizing that my input, my attitude, my choices are crucial to how my life unfolds.

"Trying" to think positively

Many people seem to have a single goal: to think positively. Positive thinking has been the subject of more self-help books and motivational speeches than any single concept in the field of personal development. What empowering impact has all of that attention about trying to think positively had on people? The reality is...almost none. Urging yourself to think positively often ignores some really stressful events of your life plus it signals to that all powerful brain that you are actually feeling negative.

This reinforces your negativity and takes you even further away from your goal of "thinking positive."

Saying that positive thinking usually doesn't work is such heresy that I may be unceremoniously drummed out of the personal development field. And yet it is mostly true.

If trying to think positive doesn't work, then what does? The answer is through taking responsibility—taking absolute responsibility for your actions, experiences and results. Taking total personal responsibility is the source of meaningful learning, growth and personal power. If I choose to adopt the victim role, then positive thinking is impossible and my self-worth plummets. When you choose to hold yourself as responsible—meaning "at cause" rather than "to blame"—your personal power and confidence will grow exponentially.

The formula is simple and often not easy: Responsibility is the source of personal power and personal power is the actual source of positive thinking.

Now knowing this and even teaching it is no guarantee that even your esteemed author is immune from the siren song of victimhood. Late fall of 1993 found me—as brilliant Master Seminar Leader and friend Dennis Becker says—"wallowing like a water buffalo" in my own self-pity. I was deep into an acrimonious divorce action and in addition to my personal pain, my children were obviously suffering. Now if you make a living teaching about responsibility, the normal behavior is that when you need to be a victim, you're very subtle, sophisticated and clever about how you express it…and I was.

One of my dear friends and coaches, Stewart Esposito, listened to my tales of woe for a long time without comment. I believe he knew he had a very tough customer to confront. Stewart knew I was way too clever, powerfully articulate and had my victim role fully justified. One day in a telephone coaching session and after just listening to me for about 60 days, he broke his silence and asked me for permission to ask a question. I gladly replied "yes."

He asked, "wouldn't it be useful to simply take responsibility for all of this?"

In that moment, I gave up all my payoffs for being a victim, took responsibility for what I did and didn't do as a husband and started a forgiveness process—of my former wife and of myself—that continues to this day. One result: a certain kind of healing for myself, for my children and for my relationship with the mother of my children. More importantly, I let go and went on with my life, went back to living my purpose, vision and values, went forward to a joyful, powerful expression of life.

Personal power and living an extraordinary life—or grungies and payoffs. What's your choice?

Ordinary People...

...confuse responsibility with blame

...allow events from the past and their reactions to them to control decisions they will make today

...believe they can will positive thinking into being

Extraordinary People...

...embody personal responsibility for their actions and results

...know that responsibility leads to personal power which naturally creates positive being and thinking

~ 19 ~

BEING RIGHT IS A LIFE-THREATENING CONDITION

I will happily die, rather than be forced to renounce what I believe.

Muntaga Tall
A religious leader of the Toucouleur people, on her refusal to
abide by a new law in Senegal banning female genital mutilation.
(*Newsweek*, February 15, 1999)

Try this. At a dinner party sometime, kick off the conversation with: "I believe that the most important objective for every human being is to be right." Then sit back and watch the fireworks. It won't take long for some bright spark to respond with something like, "Nonsense!" Or "I don't believe that!" Or "You don't know what you're talking about!" Or, maybe they'll agree with you, and join the argument on your side. Either way, people will prove your original statement to be true by in effect saying, "I'm right, and anybody who disagrees with me is wrong!"

Over a century ago, the philosopher William James noted: "Man has but one interest: to be right. That is to him the art of all arts, and all means are fair which help him to it." Put in more modern terms, we can say that human beings have an instinctual need to be right. It's not just important, it's a matter of life and death—a major part of the most powerful of all our animal instincts, the will to survive.

Although it's not so easy to see in yourself, I'm sure you can see clearly how other people view being wrong as virtually life-threatening. And, no doubt, in more primitive times, when we were threatened by savage predators (both human and non-human), being wrong or making a mistake could easily cost us our life. Yet, as with many other primitive reactions that once helped us survive, our need to be right is now destroying us personally and as a society.

"I'm right" is what arguments, the law courts, divorce and even wars are all about. The need to prove ourselves right and those who oppose us wrong destroys people and families and friendships. It actively holds us back and

Responsibility · 111

stops us from getting more done in life. Once our beliefs about ourselves and our world get established (many experts say by the age of 8 or 10) they become monumentally important to us. We will do almost anything to preserve and validate what we believe rather than look at things from a different point of view. Don't believe me? Consider this:

Would you lie to be right?

People lie to each other—and themselves—all the time to be right about what they believe. Did you ever lie to somebody because you believed that being honest would hurt their feelings? This is a belief that many of us pick up in childhood, when we tell an adult the truth and get spanked or yelled at for our honesty. In reality, as adults, most people appreciate honest feedback. However, our belief that other people can't take it makes us sacrifice our integrity.

Would you disown a close friend or loved one to be right?

Absolutely. Think of all the friendships, partnerships, families and marriages you know about that have broken up over the issue of who was right.

Would you steal to be right?

You don't think so? People do it all the time. A common example is cheating on income taxes, which of course is a form of stealing. Of course, if you tell yourself that income taxes are unfair, or that the people running the government are a bunch of crooks, or that your tax money might be wasted anyway, you have then created a perfect excuse for stealing. You get to be right. And if they audit you and catch you stealing, you get to be even more right about how unfair it is. (Some people use these same excuses to justify shoplifting, or "borrowing" things like paper, pens, pencils, paper clips and other things from their employers.)

Would you kill to be right?

No? What about war? War is all about being right. Think of the people who have died in the conflict over who's right about Communism or Capitalism. Or in wars over the centuries about which specific religious point of view was right. Do you think a nation says, "We're wrong, but we're going to war anyway?" Never. Any group going to war always has "God on our side."

Would you die to be right?

Over the course of history, millions of people have died for a "cause," a national symbol, a belief. Every day people worldwide are dying to be right about their religious, nationalistic and ethnic beliefs. Many people commit suicide. Suicide is, after all, about being right regarding beliefs such as: "Life is meaningless." "I don't deserve to go on living." "You'll be sorry when I'm gone." Or whatever belief it is that drives us to take our own lives.

To be right, would you cause your children great pain and suffering and possible psychological damage?

Millions of people do it every day. Couples who are separating and divorcing use their children as pawns, causing the children immense distress and long-term psychological damage, all to be right and make their wife or husband wrong.

Would you let your children die to be right?

There are people who do. People whose religious beliefs say that it is wrong to seek medical attention. Worse, there are people who murder their entire families. These acts are always based upon some belief. To you, the belief that would justify killing a child might seem irrational and even insane, but to the person who holds the belief, it seems logical and defensible. In other words, it is right.

Another form of being right starts even before we begin formal schooling. Many of us are conditioned from birth to search for the "right" answers. We forget that it is no accident we've got two eyes, two ears and only one mouth… and that they are most wisely used proportionally. The problem with making sure you have the right answer before you speak is this: As long as you are committed to being right about what you have already decided is true, then no new learning is possible. From a position of "I know," no truly new ideas can be created. Conversely, "I don't know" is a truly powerful position for learning, for growth and for living an extraordinary life.

Dead right or alive and wrong?

A lady I know who is usually quite rational becomes completely undone when the subject of psychiatrists comes up. She doesn't trust them. Clearly, something happened to her in the past that caused her to fear psychiatrists, suspect them of being dishonest and self-seeking, and wanting to avoid them at all costs.

I never found out what led her to develop this reaction, but it nearly cost her her life. For months she'd been complaining of headaches, nausea, sleeplessness, and generally feeling low. Doctors and specialists could find nothing wrong. Thinking it might be stress-related and perhaps even early depression, I suggested she see a psychiatrist friend of mine, to whom I'd successfully referred several others. That was at least a temporary mistake. She blew up immediately, and with a lot of defiant shouting and hand-waving, let me know that psychiatrists are a bunch of quacks.

A few months later I found out she'd been hospitalized with a mental breakdown. Happily, she was able to work through it with the guidance of a good counselor (a psychiatrist). It could have spelled disaster for her, simply because of an irrational belief. The point is, it was not irrational to her; it was very real. She was, it seemed, willing to be right and dead, rather than wrong and alive.

The self-fulfilling prophecy: "I told you so!"

Human beings are perhaps never more frightening than when they are convinced beyond doubt that they are right.

Laurens Van der Post
Lost World of the Kalahari

"I'm right" is also the basis of all self-fulfilling prophesies. For example, a man who, because of his past experiences, has come to believe that women are deceitful will constantly be on the lookout for evidence to support his belief. That's how we operate as human beings. We go around collecting evidence that we're right, even when it's self-destructive—when we'd be much better off being wrong. For example, if a man is convinced that women are deceitful, what kind of woman will he be attracted to? With what kind of woman will he ultimately have a relationship with? What kind of woman will he marry?

You guessed it: a deceitful woman. After all, only a woman who will lie to him and cheat on him will provide him with the evidence he needs to be right that women are deceitful. And when she makes a fool of him, even though it hurts, he'll collect his payoff. Once again he'll get to be right. "I told you so! Women are deceitful." His prophesy has fulfilled itself.

Here's another example. Let's say I have a belief that I can never achieve what I really want. So, why should I bother working too hard? It's pointless, since I'll never get what I want anyway. As a result, I don't try too hard or take necessary risks. Consequently, I don't succeed. I don't get what I say I want. However, I do get the Big Payoff: I get to be right. My prophesy is fulfilled (and that makes me feel smart, too).

A friend of mine has a son who was a very talented swimmer, yet he also had a deep-seated belief that he was inferior. Time and again at swim meets where he was expected to win, he would seem to swim all out—only to come in second. Unconsciously, in order to be right about the belief that he was inferior, he found ways to keep himself from winning. Each time he placed second or third, he collected more evidence to support his belief. Another perfect example of a self-fulfilling prophecy.

After he participated in our seminars, the boy realized what was going on—and suddenly began winning a lot of races. He later told his father, "Dad, I always used to hold back in a race, because I thought I needed to see how the others in front of me were swimming. Then I'd go for it in the last 25 yards and just miss winning. Now I go full blast all the way. And when I win, I feel like I deserve it. And when I don't win, I think about what I can learn from the race."

That's what I call incredible wisdom for a teenager—one well on his way to living an extraordinary life.

ORDINARY PEOPLE...

...would rather be right—even dead right—and are willing to sacrifice relationships and accomplishment in order to maintain their righteousness.

EXTRAORDINARY PEOPLE...

...let go of their need to be right and choose to live extraordinary lives of joy, contribution and accomplishment

~ 20 ~

WHO IS THAT FABULOUS PERSON HIDING UNDER YOUR IMAGE?

Death is not the greatest loss in life.
The greatest loss is what dies inside us while we live.

Norman Cousins

When we are young children, we don't have a care in the world. We laugh and cry spontaneously. We're alert and honest. We let people know when something isn't right, and we're committed to getting attention we want or need… right now!

However, it doesn't take us long to learn to abide by all the social and cultural conventions, and to conform to all the do's and the don't's of what society expects of us. As we grow, we often get put down by those around us; we get hurt and are encouraged to feel guilty or ashamed or stupid or different. Our self-esteem and self-love, once overflowing, get hammered; we start taking on beliefs about ourselves and our world, many of them negative and damaging. Our childhood experiences shape our view of who we are, and for most of us, it's a much-diminished view.

Soon, who we think we are and who we imagine we are supposed to be start coming into conflict. We discover that our hopes and dreams, thoughts and feelings, evoke reactions in others that are unpleasant or even dangerous. We learn that, in order to get along, we have to "go along." So we develop a thick shell—an image—to protect us from getting hurt, to keep us safe and to allow us to fit into society.

Who we really are takes a back seat, until pretty soon our image is all that we show and, after some time passes, all we know. Inevitably, we become our image, we adopt an identity. With our true selves hidden away, we are often in pain and holding back, afraid to come out and just be ourselves. To break out of our image, to let go of our carefully constructed identify, is to place ourselves at risk.

If you doubt this is true, take a look at teenagers. They are masters at conformity. Why? I suggest it is to avoid being hurt or humiliated. They are terrified that everyone around them will discover that who they really are as individuals is not enough. So they hide in being like everybody else else or in being different than everybody else—equally self-defeating identities.

This image-building process continues in each of us as we grow up. I think people won't like the real me, especially if they see that I am really kind and sensitive or strong and resolute, and not the cool, tough guy or cute little girl I pretend to be.

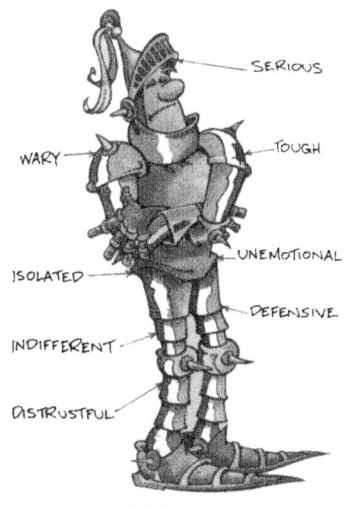

YOU AND YOUR PROTECTIVE IMAGE

THE PERSON INSIDE – THE REAL YOU

Mary Cecilia Brown rode to town on a Malibu bus
She climbed to the top of the Hollywood sign
and with the smallest possible fuss
She jumped off the letter H
'cause she did not become a star
She died in less than a minute-and-a-half
She looked a bit like Hedy Lamar.

"The Hollywood Sign"
Dory Previn

What follows is tragic. We stop risking for fear of making mistakes, fear of not fitting in, fear of being embarrassed or humiliated by saying the "wrong" thing. Our instinctive joy and boundless enthusiasm are replaced by playing it safe and looking good. Our spontaneity deserts us, and with it much of our natural creativity. Predictability replaces passion. We learn to reveal very little of who we really are and what we really feel. We sell the richness of our passionate birthright for the security of this burdensome thing called our "image." It weighs us down like a suit of medieval armor, restricting our every move, sapping our vitality and aliveness. We wander through life on automatic pilot, controlled by the need to live up to the false image that we invented.

I am reminded of the movie *Invasion of the Body Snatchers*, in which weird, plant-like creatures colonize Earth and enter human bodies, taking them over completely. We are like the "Pod People" who are the fruits of those plants: We look human, we say human things, but much of the time we are just going through the motions. In fact, many people stop allowing themselves to feel almost entirely. The aliveness and the excitement are gone, yet it's safe. Or so it seems.

One thing is certain: if we want our lives to be more exciting and rewarding, if we want our creative juices to flow freely, we need to step outside of our image and allow ourselves to be vulnerable to life. Not so safe, but we get to experience life's magic again and feel the kind of freedom we haven't known since we were children.

Ordinary People...

...are prisoners of their image, their identity, and therefore lack spontaneity and genuine connection to others

Extraordinary People...

...are vulnerable, risking and ultimately free

~ 21 ~

TIME TO WAKE UP! YOU'VE GOT THE WRONG GOAL

*I could have missed the pain
But I'd have had to miss the dance.*

"The Dance"
Performed by Garth Brooks
Written by Tony Arata

Let's look at our image in a slightly different way.

We develop an image because it's the only way we know to protect ourselves, to survive our parents' demands to conform and be like them. As I said earlier, when we were little, we were totally honest. We hadn't learned yet how to lie in order to survive. Remember when you were five years old and you told your auntie Doris—in front of a room full of visitors—that she had "lots of funny wrinkles on her face and blue lines on her legs?" One way or another, you got whacked by your parents for saying that, for being honest. When you went to school and told your teacher she was fat, you were just being honest. And it didn't work in terms of you getting the approval and support that you wanted and needed from these most important people in your young life.

Pretty soon you figured out that, if you were to survive in this world, if you wanted to get by, you'd have to stop being honest. You'd have to be polite and tell the acceptable lies. Before long the lies became central to maintaining your image. Being polite and surviving was all that mattered. Who you really are became lost, buried beneath the image you created to survive. In fact, you gradually reached a point where you could not tell the difference between your image and you. You became your identity. It was all you knew.

Ever since then your goal has been to survive. And in the process you may have lost touch with the real you. You may have thrown away, not only your spontaneity and joy and passion for living, you threw away the only thing that really matters: yourself. You traded in who you are, for survival. Because, after all, the only thing that matters is to survive, right?

Wrong. It does not matter a damn what you do to survive, because it will not help. You are not going to survive. You are going to die. We all are. So, in giving away who you really are in the name of survival, you have unwittingly sold your soul. You have lost the only opportunity you will ever have to experience the incredible joy and fulfillment of YOUR LIFE as it really is in the only life we can actually experience—this one, this time, this collection of successive moments of now.

That's the bad news. The good news? You can get it back. You have a choice. Are you going to live to survive, or survive to live?

Life is hard, ain't it?

*Life is a gamble at terrible odds—if it was
a bet, you wouldn't take it.*
Tom Stoppard

"Life is difficult." So begins the popular book, *The Road Less Traveled*, by Dr. M. Scott Peck. This is not news to any of us, is it? We all know life is hard. Don't we? This explains the source and popularity of the bumper sticker:

"Life's a bitch and then you die"

It turns out, in fact, that we don't know that. As Dr. Peck points out, many of us hold the unrealistic expectation that life should be easy and fair and just and comfortable. As a result, the normal ups and downs, joys and pains, of everyday life show up as a living hell of disappointment and frustration.

Spiritual and philosophical leaders have been telling us for a couple of thousand years that our expectations are what create all the hopelessness in our lives, and we still don't get it.

Our crazy creation called expectations

Why go through life being sad or angry, or feeling defeated because reality does not conform to our expectations? Wouldn't it make more sense to change our attitudes, beliefs and expectations to fit the way that life is? Well, it might make more sense, but it is not always how we act. As long as human beings are future-oriented, we will generate notions of what has not yet been created, which means we will continue to have expectations.

The challenge we face is distinguishing between useful envisioning of the future as something to be created, versus expecting things to evolve according to our preconceptions—and then feeling victimized when events don't unfold as we expected.

> "Expectations are real killers. They are setups for disappointment. Often, because of our expectations, we are completely oblivious to what is really going on in a situation. Because we are so wedded to what we think should be happening, or what we don't want to happen, we don't see what is happening…
>
> Expectations also keep us in illusion. We set up our expectations for someone, we project them onto the other person, and then we start reacting to our expectations as if they were real. Expectations and the illusion of control are intimately linked."
>
> Dr. Anne Wilson Schaef
> *Meditations for Women Who Do Too Much*

Unlike our visions, our expectations are often inventions of self-torture. Whereas many of our beliefs work for us and keep us safe, expectations, especially those we have of other people, invariably bring us disappointment. They set us up to feel victimized by the way things actually are.

> "I got up on my feet and went over to the bowl in the corner and threw cold water on my face. After a while I felt a little better, but very little. I needed a drink, I needed a lot of life insurance, I needed a vacation, I needed a home in the country. What I had was a coat, a hat and gun. I put them on and went out of the room."
>
> Raymond Chandler's detective
Philip Marlowe

Remember the movie *Dead Poet's Society*? The film gave a terrifyingly real look at the destructive force of expectations, when the successful physician father of a boy at an exclusive boarding school demanded that his son abandon his passionate desire to become a professional actor and follow in his father's footsteps to become a doctor. The boy kills himself, a direct result of his father's expectations, which completely ignored the deep and strongly felt wants and needs of his son.

In one of our seminars, a man in his late fifties related to the group how his once-close relationship with his 18-year-old daughter had been shattered. She had been a top high school basketball player, and he was her coach. Together, they lived and breathed the game. His expectation to see her become a star in the professional ranks began when she was just six years old. All went according to plan until, just six months before I met him, his daughter announced without warning that she was giving up the game because she was no longer interested in it. Her father was devastated. Arguments and fights ensued and, in no time, they stopped speaking to each other. Then, she moved out of the family home.

With some questioning and coaching in our seminar, the man began to see that the problem was his, not his daughter's. He'd invented expectations for his daughter and forced them onto her. These expectations had little to do with who she was or what she really wanted from life. What he had described as being "good" for her was really only good for him, yet he had not been able to see it. Like any child who wants to please her father, she did the best she could to follow his program for her life. Finally, the gap between who she really was and this image she had acquired largely as a result of her father's expectations became so great that she could no longer stand the strain. For the father it was painful to realize that his expectations of his daughter had created the rift between them, and put their loving relationship at risk.

ORDINARY PEOPLE...

...believe they actually are their image and lose touch with their authentic self and their dreams

EXTRAORDINARY PEOPLE...

...put their own or other's expectations in the proper context and live their dreams without limitation

~ 22 ~

WISHFUL THINKING VERSUS REALITY

*In life, you either have the results you want, or you have
reasons to explain why you don't have them.
If you have the results, you don't need the reasons.*

From the Extraordinary Living Seminar

I've pointed out before our human tendency to try to look good at all costs, which involves finding somebody or something else to blame whenever things don't turn out the way we want them to. This tendency can all too easily lead us down the road to playing victim, which blocks our energy and limits our effectiveness, not to mention all the grungy feelings with which we burden ourselves. What works is to be responsible, and to operate from the point of view that the results I create come from my choices and my actions—100 percent.

An easy way to remind yourself of this is by asking yourself the question: "Am I satisfied with my reasons or my results?" When I have the results I say I'm committed to, I don't need any reasons (excuses, rationalizations, justifications) to explain why I don't have them. And when I don't have the results I want, my reasons are simply a way to shift the blame from me to somebody or something else, to play victim, in other words. Although this is easier and less painful in the short run, in the long run I end up giving up my power and self-esteem, like all victims.

To be more effective, I need to give up my excuses and look honestly at how my own choices and actions have created my results, without sinking into guilt and self-blame. The real choice is between temporary pleasure and permanent pain (from avoiding what my results tell me); or, temporary pain and permanent pleasure (from confronting my results honestly).

The "reasons or results" question is also a useful reminder that the only way to tell what my real intentions are in any situation is to look at my results. Results tell me what I'm really up to and as I've said before, we're all good at lying to ourselves when we don't want to deal with the truth. Results don't lie. That's why when people say they are confused about their priorities, it's almost always productive to ask them to look and see what's actually important to them "based on results."

How's it going—based on results?

I'm reminded of a young woman (I'll call her Jane) in one of our seminars who, on the first night, shared that her purpose in attending was to find out what was keeping her from getting started on her chosen career path. "I know what I want to do," she said, "but I keep postponing it. I want to figure out why."

I asked her to tell us a little about herself. She said she was married to an international airline pilot, and that in order to be with her husband, she traveled to Europe or South America one or two weeks a month. "Otherwise, I'd never see him," she said. "That's why I can't have a regular job."

"So, what do you do when you're not traveling with your husband?" I asked.

"Since I was married seven years ago, I've mostly just been playing tennis in the mornings with the other airline 'widows' whose husbands are away, going to coffee with them, shopping…and working out to keep myself in good shape."

"Sounds nice," I said. "You said before that you know what you want to do in terms of a career. What is it, if you don't mind my asking?"

"I want to work with disabled children," she said. "It's been my dream since before I got married."

"I hear what you're saying, Jane," I said, "and maybe before this seminar is over there'll be a shift in you so that working with disabled children becomes your real priority. However, for the last seven years, what are you committed to, based on results?"

"I don't know," she said.

"Well, based on what you've been telling us, what seems to be important to you is your marriage." I said. "Being with your husband and being a good 'airline wife' as you put it. It's not right or wrong, it's simply the reality, based on results. You're obviously an intelligent and competent woman and if working with disabled children was really a priority for you, I'm sure you would have found a way in seven years to do it, at least part-time. Based on results, something else has been more important."

"But I really do want to find a way to help handicapped children," she said. "It's just that I don't know where to start. And I really don't have any formal training. I feel like I need to go back to school and get a degree in how to work with disabled children. If I start working on a degree and my husband gets relocated to another country…" She then fell silent.

"Clearly, you've got lots of reasons why you don't have what you say you want, Jane," I said. "It's a good illustration of what we've been talking about. In life, we either have the results we want, or we have the reasons to explain why we haven't achieved them. All your reasons have you stuck, they just create a kind of fog wherein you cannot see clearly. So you find ways to distract yourself from following your dream, like playing tennis and going shopping, when what you say you want to do is make a difference with kids."

"That's very clear and it feels true to me," she said.

"Then it's time to go for the results you want," I said, "and leave the reasons behind."

The message was and is clear. In life you have either the results you want or excuses to explain why you don't have them. Both cannot occupy the same space. You can always tell the losers' locker room: It's the one filled with reasons like, "bad referees," "it was an off night for us," "I wasn't feeling a hundred percent today," etc. The winners don't need to say anything.

I love speaking to sales teams and have done so all over the world. I often get permission to attend a regular sales meeting prior to my speech and one learning from that practice is that no matter where I am geographically and even if I don't speak the local language, a pattern is apparent. Most sales meetings begin with a report on results by all present. You can measure the emotional health of the organization and the people in it by simply timing the presentations. If they are brief, you've got a great organization with people who are creating results. If the presentations are lengthy, you've got problems — people are sharing reasons, not results.

People who take responsibility for all they create are able to quickly sort truth from fiction in their lives, and in the communication they're receiving from those around them, by using the simple litmus test of "based on results." Wishing and hoping, reasons and excuses will never tell you the truth. If you say you intend to have a happy marriage, have you got one? If you say you want to earn a degree from a good university, have you done it? If you say you want ten million dollars, do you have the money? If you don't have what you say you want, then how come? You've either got the results you say you want, or you have reasons to explain why not. Developing a rigorous and honest relationship with results moves you powerfully toward creating your extraordinary life.

So, how's it going for you? Based on results?

~ 23 ~

THERE IS NO HOPE

The phone rings. I am not amused. This is not my favorite way to wake up. My favorite way to wake up is to have a certain French movie star whisper to me softly at two thirty in the afternoon that if I want to get to Sweden in time to pick up my Nobel Prize for Literature I had better ring for breakfast. This occurs rather less often than one might wish.

Fran Lebowitz

To one degree or another, we're all experts in hoping and wishing. As instant problem-solvers, hoping and wishing have no equal. They instantly push to the back burner whatever it is you want to accomplish, inviting procrastination, and without the down-side of having to feel guilty about being a procrastinator. You get to avoid risk, failure and self-doubt. Wishing and hoping are often self-delusion, and by surrendering to their seductive song we get to remain safe in our comfort zone. We don't have to change, we can hope instead.

A favorite expression of mine is, "There is no hope." Please don't misinterpret me. I'm not saying that we shouldn't be hopeful of a successful future for ourselves and a better world for all. We are creatures for whom optimism about the future is vital to our well-being. No, I mean "hope" in the sense of wishful thinking. If you want to accomplish big goals in your life, then consider deleting that particular use of the word "hope" from your vocabulary.

Hanging out in hope, in the sense of dwelling in a state of wishful thinking, doesn't accomplish anything. In fact, for many of us, hoping takes the place of risking, commitment, and hard work—so that hoping gets in the way of achieving what we want. I might hope to wake up tomorrow and find a Mercedes Benz in my garage. Unless I'm willing to do what it takes to put one there, my hoping is just a way to substitute fantasy for reality.

Maybe you're *trying* too hard

Along with "hope," "try" is another word to eliminate from your vocabulary. "I'll try" is an excuse, a back door exit in case something doesn't turn out the way you'd planned. It allows you to give less than 100 percent and then stop when the going gets rough. After all, you said you'd "try," and that's exactly what you did. You never promised to actually accomplish anything.

Think of the well-worn story of Thomas Edison and the light bulb: If Edison had been "trying" to invent the light bulb, he would have given up long before he finally achieved his goal after many thousands of failures. Edison wasn't "trying." He was committed to do whatever it was going to take to get the job done.

Here's a simple exercise. Try to pick up a pen or pencil from your table. OK…did you pick it up? Great, but that's not trying, that's doing it. You didn't "try" to pick it up, you acted and picked it up. There is a huge difference.

If you are alert to it, you will hear people say, "I'll try" whenever they're looking for an excuse to be late, or for doing less than an excellent job. If you ask a printer to have a brochure printed for you on a certain day and he says, "I'll try," can you count on the brochure being ready? Or, if you're mountain climbing and you shout to your climbing partner to let out more rope, and he yells back, "I'll try!" will it fill you with confidence?

By eliminating unconscious uses of "try" and "wish" and "hope" from your life, you'll find that things get done quicker and with remarkable ease. Life will become more positive and you'll be more effective. In this life you can either commit yourself to being a "doer," or you can "try." People who try have reasons and excuses. Doers have results.

~ 24 ~

REDEFINING SUCCESS

Far better it is to dare mighty things, to win glorious triumphs even though checkered by failure, than to rank with those poor spirits who neither enjoy nor suffer much because they live in the gray twilight that knows neither victory nor defeat.

Theodore Roosevelt

In February 1998, a friend of this book's producer, Peter Sherwood, set out to realize a dream he'd had since he was an idealistic 17-year-old. He'd read an exciting account of Sir Ernest Shackleton's epic open-boat journey in 1916 from Antarctica to remote South Georgia island, and how Shackleton had crossed the island to get help and rescue his men stranded on a barren rock some 800 miles away.

Shackleton's remarkable climb across South Georgia was the first time the island had been traversed. Only a handful of people have done it since. After a thirty-five year wait, Peter's friend finally made the trip with an enthusiastic small group, led by an experienced Antarctic and Himalayan climbing guide, Dave Hahn. Hahn received world media attention in 1999 when his team on Mt. Everest found the body of legendary climber, George Leigh Mallory, lost on the mountain in 1924. On South Georgia island, Hahn's group spent a week battling hurricane winds and whiteouts in an effort to follow in Shackleton's footsteps. It wasn't to be. Almost out of supplies, they finally made a short crossing of the island and called in the ship to pick them up.

When Dave Hahn announced that they would have to give up on their attempt, one of the group became particularly resentful at having, as he said, "...come all this way to fail." Hahn seemed relaxed and smiled at the man. "Hey, I'm at least as disappointed about this as you are. We did all we could. To continue in this lousy visibility over uncharted and crevassed glaciers, with hardly any food or fuel, would be asking for trouble. And if we get into trouble down here, there's no rescue service. No helicopters, no nothin'. Anyway, this is not a discussion. However, what I can do for you is suggest that you change your definition of success."

There's no such thing as failure

That sums up my own view. There is no such thing as failure. There are only results. Failure is the judgment we choose to place on the event. Your results are there for you to learn from. What matters is not your judgment of success or failure, but your experience, how you interpret the results you've produced.

If the climber who complained had stopped to think about it, he would have been more keenly aware that his legendary hero, Shackleton, did not achieve even one of his original goals as an explorer. To most people, that should have made him a monumental failure. Yet it was in falling short of his objectives that his epic journeys and international acclaim as a great leader were born.

> "If you can meet with Triumph and Disaster
> And treat those two impostors just the same..."
>
> Rudyard Kipling
> *"If"*

Our culture tends to label everybody and everything as either a success or a failure, a winner or a loser. I often wonder how the one winner and the 58,000 losers in the Boston Marathon feel about that? I can't imagine even one of those runners thinking of himself as a loser. I believe that for every one of them, to run the race well is to succeed. To push forward until perhaps you are unable to walk is to win. And perhaps the greatest victory of all is the bringing together, in a spirit of friendship and commitment, 58,000 runners, thousands of volunteers and the hundreds of thousands more who cheer them on. I call all of these people winners, and I believe most of them see it the same way. Of course, these are extraordinary people, or they wouldn't be committed to running a marathon in the first place. They are actually choosing to defy a culture which celebrates being a spectator—as contrasted with actually participating—and often communicates that anything other than first place constitutes ignominious defeat. In Dr. Wayne W. Dyer's book, *Pulling Your Own Strings*, he says:

> "You do not need victories over other human beings to control yourself from within and be fulfilled. Only losers need to win, since needing to win implies that you can't be happy unless you defeat someone else out there. If you can't be happy without someone else whom you must defeat, then you are being controlled by that person, which makes you the ultimate loser, since people who are controlled by others are psychological slaves.... You can surely look at winning as something terrific to achieve, but you should be even more certain that your essence as a person does not depend on the achievement."

Good bear, bad bear

This is a simple story of how we human beings outsmart ourselves, and why bears are wiser than us in a number of ways.

It's an early Spring morning in the forest. Flowers are beginning to bloom, the sun is high in the sky, and the snowy remains of winter fill the streams in a growing torrent. The air is crisp and clear. Deep in the woods a huge grizzly bear awakens from his long winter hibernation. He stretches, growls and looks around. His first thought is food. Rising on all fours he ambles over to a nearby log, rotten with decay. Sniffing around it, he finally lifts one end of the old log searching for something to eat. He finds worms and insects in abundance. Quickly he eats and moves on to a second log where he repeats the exercise. At the third and fourth logs, however, there is no food. So he wanders off down to the stream to try his massive paw at fishing. There, he will catch some fish. Or he won't. Apart from being hungry or not, whether he catches a fish, or finds grubs and insects under a log is all the same to the bear.

For most people, however, the experience is very different. Imagine a human being in the bear's situation. Typically, we would lift up the log, find food and quietly claim success. Then, when we lifted up logs and found nothing, we'd call it failure. So, on the one hand we lift the log and we say we are successful; on the other hand, we lift the log and we say that we have failed.

We humans ascribe a meaning, a significance, to "lifting the log," which is a metaphor for the way we approach just about every activity we undertake. It starts when we are children. When we "succeed" at something, the implication is that we are "good." And what do good people get? They get rewarded. When we don't "succeed" at something, we are told we have "failed," and the implication is that we are "bad." And bad people get punished.

The bear does not do that. The bear does not succeed or fail. He is simply out there looking for food. If he finds it, he eats. If he doesn't find it, he moves on. There are no other meanings in these actions for the bear, so why should there be for us? We human beings invented the labels of "good" and "bad," "success" and "failure." So if we invented the labels, then surely we can wake up, make some more conscious choices and live our lives in a more healthy, fulfilling way. We have also been playing this success/failure game for a very long time. So changing it, while simple, is not always easy.

~ 25 ~

LEARNING TO LOVE YOUR MISTAKES

We would rather be ruined than change;
We would rather die in our dread
Than climb the cross of the moment
And let our illusions die.

W.H. Auden

The black-and-white separation of success and failure begins very early in life and is often formalized in school. And although schools are becoming more aware of the damage done by labeling a child as a success or a failure at an early age, they still reinforce the notion that you must always have the "right" answer. Only those with the right answer put up their hands to respond to a question. The idea of not daring to fail carries right through to the management of large corporations, where executives will often not commit themselves until they're sure they know the "right" thing to say.

Robert Louis Stevenson said, "Give me the young man who has enough brains to make a fool of himself." And if you are not prepared to make a fool of yourself, it means you're playing it safe, hiding out by being unimaginative and unoriginal, and repeating what you think everyone wants to hear.

All scientific research is based on making mistakes: finding out what doesn't work as you move toward discovering what does work. Mistakes are what babies make when they're learning to walk. Imagine criticizing a baby and telling her, "You're wrong!" every time she wobbles to her feet, only to fall down for the twentieth time. Wobbling to your feet is called progress. And if the Wright brothers had been frightened of making mistakes, your last flight to Europe might have been in a hot air balloon.

How does this apply in our daily lives? Think about your work. If you play it safe and avoid taking risks in order to look good in your company, you detract from the organization's effectiveness, to say nothing of your own professional progress and personal satisfaction. And think how badly it affects the spawning of good ideas—your ideas—so many of which are born from what seemed to be ridiculous suggestions. Progressive companies positively promote this sort of input from their staff because it inevitably creates a wealth of new thinking and energy. It allows people to be acknowledged and to feel good about the creative process and their contribution to it. And it results in employees who appreciate their company for its supportive environment.

Breaking free of our ingrained beliefs in this domain is very challenging. I remember struggling to learn Japanese while a resident in Japan. It was clear that this was important to me for generating better communication and better relationships, personally and professionally. It was also clear that the number one barrier to becoming more fluent was my reluctance to sound foolish, my fear of making mistakes, of looking like a failure. The result, I didn't get the practice I needed for fluency.

The young son of a friend of mine came home from school one day looking depressed. He told his father he scored only 12 out of 20 that day in a science test, making eight mistakes, while his best friend had a perfect score. His dad asked him what his friend had learned in the science class that day. The boy thought for a while and replied, "Nothing." "Right," his father said. "And what did you learn?" His son looked up and smiled. "Eight new things."

Everything we enjoy in society is a direct result of the accumulated learning derived from millions of mistakes. No mistakes, no progress. Yet we still look at making a mistake as though it were embarrassing, wrong, an act bordering on sin. If you're making mistakes, it means you're doing new things, taking risks, stretching yourself. You're growing, learning. And isn't the journey, the experience, not the destination, what life is all about?

Perfection: in pursuit of the impossible

So many people spend (or often waste) their lives in search of perfection. In reality, perfection is usually an unattainable fantasy and, of course, each person defines for themselves what "perfection" means. In setting out to reach perfection, we almost always limit and restrict ourselves. When your objective is to be perfect at something, you're going to try to minimize risk, minimize failure, minimize mistakes of any kind. Even worse, you'll be unwilling to attempt anything new or unfamiliar. Why would a perfectionist try something new when he's not certain he can be perfect at it?

If I were a perfectionist I would never have taken up skiing at 45 years old. How could I suffer the embarrassment of being a beginner and a novice, of looking like a fool on the slopes compared to more experienced skiers? Today I'm proud to say that I am probably the worst skier in the Aspen Mountain Club. What's most important to me is that I am ON THE MOUNTAIN and learning!

Imagine wanting to be a perfect golfer. It would make the game impossible, which is why a true perfectionist should never start playing in the first place. A true perfectionist would have to shoot a perfect round, every time. I don't know much about the game, but I do know that the object is to shoot the lowest possible score. Therefore, a perfect round of golf must be 18 consecutive holes-in-one. I'm not a betting man, but I'll give you whatever odds you want on that one never happening.

If we only began projects that we were sure we could complete perfectly, then little would get done at all. Wanting perfection means doing what you're already good at. The constant striving for it only creates frustration. And if you did achieve what you've defined as perfection, you'd quickly change your definition and aim even higher. That's what perfectionists do.

On the surface, pursuing perfection appears to be a way to feel good about myself by maintaining high standards and achieving outstanding results. On an unconscious level, exactly the opposite is going on. Why would I pursue an impossible, unattainable goal like perfection? Precisely because when I don't attain it, it allows me to feel inadequate, over and over again. Since I never achieve my lofty goals, I experience continual disappointment. And each time I do, I get to be right about my basic belief in my own inadequacy.

Another version of the perfectionist game sounds something like: "I can't do it perfectly, so why start at all?" The name of this game is to avoid ever doing anything new or different. The payoff? Never having to risk or change. You are not perfect. So what? Neither is anyone else. Imperfections are like gravity: there when you go to bed at night and there when you get up in the morning. You can bitch and moan about gravity, but what's the point? Like everyone else on the planet, you too have your nerdy qualities. You might as well fall in love with them. They are not going away.

ORDINARY PEOPLE...

...focus on reason, excuses and their "story" for not having what they say they want

...hang out in "hope" and "try" to be successful

...hold a narrow and ultimately self-defeating definition of success and failure

EXTRAORDINARY PEOPLE...

...focus on results, on mileposts passed, on a non-self-critical reality

...do it. Learn. Do it again.

...realize life is a journey and never stop learning

~ 26 ~

EMBRACING CHANGE: THE TRULY DIFFICULT HUG

It is not the strongest of the species that survive, nor the most intelligent, but the one most responsive to change.

Charles Darwin
British Naturalist

Alan Watts said, "It has been said that to define is to kill, and if the wind were to stop for one second for us to catch hold of it, it would cease to be wind. The same is true of life. Perpetually things and events are moving and changing; we cannot call back past time or keep forever a passing sensation. Once we try to do this all we have is a dead memory; the reality is not there, and no satisfaction can be found in it."

Continual change is the only constant in the universe, so you might imagine that we sophisticated human beings would by now be getting the hang of it. You would of course be wrong. People hate change. It demands discomfort and a leap into the unknown, and we do not like either one. Even for those special individuals who make a life of high adventure, stepping off the edge into the void is always a major challenge.

We will suffer all sorts of unnecessary and self-imposed agonies to avoid making deep and lasting changes in our lives. Why? Why would we continue to do things we know don't work, or could even kill us? Why do we intelligent human beings continue to act so irrationally?

The answer is simple: making any significant change in our lives means changing not just our actions, but also our beliefs. As I've said before, you and I would rather die—literally—than give up our beliefs, including the ones that are limiting and self-defeating. As human history shows only too clearly, people everywhere will die for their beliefs, even trivial ones and even ones that conflict with other beliefs (like the sanctity of all life) within the same belief system. Uncountable lives have been lost warring over the primacy, the righteousness, of the beliefs behind Jewish, Muslim, Christian, Hindu and other religious faiths—all of which hold love and peace among people as central to their philosophies. Our beliefs are simply organizing structures we've chosen, many no longer appropriate to creating the lives we want, until we inject them with do-or-die importance.

So, if you want to make positive changes for the better, be prepared to give up some of your cherished beliefs, those notions that you took on board so long ago that you probably can't even remember why. The incontrovertible truth is that you can change your limiting beliefs because…you created them in the first place. Getting that truth and acting on it will change your experience of life from ordinary to extraordinary. Simple, and again, sometimes not easy.

~ 27 ~

Everybody Wants to Go to Heaven, but Nobody Wants to Die

Happiness is beneficial to the body but it is grief that develops the powers of the mind.

Marcel Proust

By its very nature, change is noticeable; it is uncomfortable and often painful or it wouldn't be called change. Throughout our lives, our most significant learnings seem to arrive via this route, through pain and affliction. The mythologies of every culture on earth are full of stories of heroes and heroines who endure painful trials and tribulations in order to achieve wisdom and insight.

Change is painful. That's just the way things are. It's just one reason we human beings will go to extraordinary lengths to stay in our rut, holding on tightly to all the pain of the past. And why not, if change is so unpleasant? The problem is, in our frantic efforts to avoid short-term pain, we also avoid self-knowledge and greater awareness, and invite confusion and long-term suffering. Again, the choice is clear: temporary pain and permanent pleasure or temporary pleasure and permanent pain.

Noted British journalist Malcolm Muggeridge wrote:

> "Contrary to what might be expected, I look back on experiences that at the time seemed especially desolate and painful. I now look back on them with particular satisfaction. Indeed, I can say with complete truthfulness that everything I have learned in my seventy-five years in this world, everything that has truly enhanced and enlightened my existence has been through affliction and not through happiness whether pursued or attained. In other words...if it were possible to eliminate affliction from our earthly existence by means of some drug or other medical mumbo-jumbo, the result would not be to make life delectable, but to make it too banal and trivial to be endurable."

Nobody wants to be in pain and torment. But did you ever experience a great insight following a traumatic event? Something that gave you a horrible or terrifying jolt and confronted you with some new and difficult questions, like the loss of a loved one, a severe physical injury or disability, a career gone wrong, a bout of depression or a job lost? Rotten stuff, yet enlightenment and self-knowledge are often found precisely within these painful experiences.

Paradoxically, perhaps, there often seems nothing enduring to be gained in terms of meaningful life change purely from leisure, from having a great time. If you or I could redesign the world we'd certainly do it very differently, so that every time we took a magic vacation at some tropical paradise we would return full of more wisdom than the *World Encyclopedia of Philosophical Quotations*. Until then, we are well advised to accept the reality that the great lessons in life often come to us through some form of extreme hardship. The conclusion here is that when you get "slapped upside the head" (my language here betraying my West Virginia birth), it's a great idea to say to yourself and anyone else that will listen…"Whoopee!!! Another learning opportunity!"

However, since we tend to avoid and resist pain, instead of embracing it and experiencing it fully, most of us as adults end up carrying around with us significant amounts of dysfunctional pain from the past. All healing begins with being willing to experience this past pain, and then from the process of letting it go. If we keep it buried, avoiding the pain through alcohol or work or romance or one of the many other ways we have of distracting ourselves, we set ourselves up for a low level of pain that lasts a lifetime. In other words, we set ourselves up for a life without joy, a life of survival.

Real life experience tells us a low level of constant pain is still a great deal of pain, when added of over the years of a lifetime. Viktor Frankl, in *Man's Search for Meaning*, noted:

> "…a man's suffering is similar to the behavior of gas. If a certain quantity of gas is pumped into an empty chamber, it will fill the chamber completely and evenly, no matter how big the chamber. Thus suffering completely fills the human soul and conscious mind, no matter whether the suffering is great or little. Therefore, the 'size' of human suffering is absolutely relative."

One adult choice we all have is to confront and deal with the pain from our past. Even healthy and successful people often carry, like a knapsack filled with rocks, past guilt, shame, regrets, blame—all accumulated in the normal process of living life and now preventing them from embracing and living a truly extraordinary life. We always have a choice: We can opt for a continuation of a low level of pain and numbness that lasts a lifetime. Or, we can have the sometimes difficult, sometimes very easy experience of facing ourselves and the pain of the past, seeing and feeling it through new eyes, letting it go and being done with it.

People who choose the latter strategy experience the liberation and joy that such a major release can bring, and more importantly, their relationship with life itself is renewed. Once again, they see the world through fresh eyes.

ORDINARY PEOPLE...

...fear change and see it as an enemy to be fought or at least resisted

...would rather be right—even dead right—than succeed

...prefer short-term pleasure even if the price is permanent pain

EXTRAORDINARY PEOPLE...

...embrace change, relax and flow with life's ups and downs

...continually re-examine any belief that gets in the way of living the life they want, their extraordinary life

...will accept short-term pain if it leads to long-term, permanent pleasure, joy and satisfaction

~ 28 ~

YOU'RE LIVING LIFE BACK TO FRONT

*The bean counters who create the national
income statistics know the price of everything
and the value of nothing.*

Wayne Muller
(*Forbes*, October 18, 1999)

The reason you and I work hard is not for the cash itself, but the experiences we believe money will bring us: everything from security, freedom, status, respect, power, self-esteem, success, friendship, sex and a lot more free time. Right?

Well, let's see. First, what is money? Money is simply dirty pieces of paper with pictures of dead people on it. In and of itself, money is worthless—and useless, except maybe for starting a fire. It is simply a vehicle for storing and exchanging value. Money can serve as a hindrance or as an advantage in our journey to live an extraordinary life. It's another belief based choice. We are culturally programmed to think that money automatically generates experiences which will make us happy. We are bombarded daily with loud messages from advertising media, trying to convince us to buy things with money that will give us personal satisfaction, so we can live "the good life." *Time* magazine quoted Bill Bradley as saying

> 'The Dow Jones is at record heights. But such numbers are not the measure of all things. They do not measure what is in our heads and our hearts. They do not measure a young girl's smile or a little boy's first handshake or a grandmother's pride. They tell us little about the magic of a good marriage or the satisfaction of a life led true to its own values.
>
> "Robert Kennedy said it better in February 1968: he referred to the fact that the gross national product was rising above $800 billion a year but said that figure does not measure 'the health of our youth, the quality of their education or the joy of their play...the beauty of our poetry or the strength of our mar-

riages, the intelligence of our public debate or the integrity of our public officials. It measures everything, in short, except that which makes life worthwhile.'"

Arthur Schlesinger Jr.
Time, November 22, 1999

Let's take a common example. Here's how many of us think: "If I get a new Mercedes, I'll feel confident and secure, everybody will respect me and look up to me, my boss will promote me, I'll attract a sexy new girlfriend, and then I'll really be happy." In other words, getting the money to buy the car I really want will automatically bring with it the experiences I need to be happy.

Money is not an experience

We think lots of money will give us the power to have all kinds of things we don't have now—which will make us happy. But is it true? Let's look deeper. How about...

Security?

If I have money, I'll definitely feel safe and secure, right? Maybe. For many of us, the more money we have, the more insecure we feel. We may doubt who our true friends are, or whether a prospective wife or husband really loves us for ourselves. Think of billionaire Howard Hughes. He became so paranoid about people trying to steal his money that he spent the last years of his life holed up on the top floor of a Las Vegas hotel, never so much as opening a window. With all that money, he felt anything but secure.

Freedom?

Money represents the clear possibility of increasing freedom; however, it's more likely that the more wealth we have, the more time it takes to manage it. And the more we worry about losing it. We need a bank vault for jewelry, a security system for our home. Is that freedom, or loss of freedom? Think about it: At what period in your life did you feel most free? At the time when you had the most money? Or when you were young, with no responsibilities tying you down, able to come and go as you pleased? For many people, money becomes a burden, a barrier to freedom.

Status?

Certainly many people think so—but in fact it's often not the case. Some drug dealers, for example, are extremely wealthy, but they have little status. They have to hide their identities to keep from being arrested. There are countless celebrities whose status is clearly temporary. And some rich people completely conceal the fact that they are wealthy. The best-selling book, *The Millionaire Next Door*, described how most wealthy people live very ordinary lives and refrain from showing their wealth in any way that would draw attention to themselves. They have little status. And some people whom we hold as being at the top of the status chart had no money at all. Think of Abraham Lincoln or Martin Luther King.

Respect?

Are you kidding? Many wealthy people are despised for their stinginess, or hated for being ruthless. Yet people like the late Mother Teresa, who lived in poverty, are loved and respected by millions the world over. There's nothing wrong with having money, however nobody has ever earned respect for money alone.

Power?

There are people with power and very little money, just as there are people with a lot of money and very little real power. Mahatma Gandhi was enormously powerful, and he was virtually penniless—and there are plenty of people with money who feel weak and helpless. Money does not automatically bring us power.

Self-esteem?

It can't be bought, in spite of the fact that there are a lot of people trying. Self-esteem comes from being in integrity with myself, from being proud of who I really am and the contribution I make. You can read in the paper every day about wealthy people with no self-esteem who commit suicide (Marilyn Monroe is a famous example).

Friendship?

Money can actually get in the way of friendship. Friends we had before we got wealthy can't afford to keep up. And our willingness to pay their way often alienates them further. Often, we are often never quite sure if our "new" friends would be there for us if we were poor.

Love?

Yeah, right. Maybe by the hour in Tijuana or Bangkok or by the night with the "platinum diggers" at the Caribou Club in Aspen.

Money is just a symbol; it is not an experience. Mastering the right relationship with money can contribute to creating an extraordinary life…and it doesn't guarantee it. The verdict is in, and has been for centuries, and often we are not listening. What we need to be happy, to be secure and free and satisfied, you and I already have. What's more, we've had it all our lives. The secret is on the inside, not the outside.

Dissatisfaction, and why your car wheel is round

Something in addition to freedom of choice distinguishes human beings from animals—we are never satisfied. As we evolved as a species, our dissatisfaction grew. First, all we wanted was a crude form of shelter while we hunted for something to eat.

However, we were dissatisfied with hunting and gathering, so we developed agriculture. We were dissatisfied with life in a cave, so we developed houses, then villages, towns and cities.

Our insatiable desire to make life easier and more comfortable, led to inventions, to the industrial revolution and to the information age. We were dissatisfied with the state of our health and rampaging diseases, so we developed medicine and kept improving its quality. Dissatisfaction with our moral condition continues to lead us to improve human rights and the judicial system.

> Beaver: "Gee, there's something wrong with just about everything, isn't there Dad?"
> Ward: "Just about, Beav."
>
> The TV Show "Leave it to Beaver"

Look around you now and you'll see it's true: In almost every sphere of human life, we are in a constant state of dissatisfaction. In our quest to feel satisfied we miss the point: Dissatisfaction is a gift. It is what drives that very human need to feel more contented and fulfilled. We were dissatisfied with being earth-bound. We wanted to fly. We did. Now we fly everywhere, cheaply, at 600 MPH, at the speed of sound and beyond. Now we want to go faster. A few short years ago we were enthralled with the idea of having a personal computer. We got one. A few weeks later we wanted to change it because it was too slow and had limited features.

And not content with life on earth, we spend billions of dollars to go into outer space. We like to imagine our goal is to feel satisfied, but a perpetual state of total satisfaction does not seem to be within the realm of possibility for people.

That is good news. If we were designed to be in a constant state of satisfaction, then you might still be wondering why the square wheel on your bullock cart made for such a bumpy ride.

Does this mean we can never be happy? No, not at all. It simply means that we need to understand that human nature is not designed to be completely satisfied—at least not for very long. We thrive on new challenges. As soon as we reach the top of one hill, we look ahead to the next hill to climb. Once we fully acknowledge that particular part of our nature, we can then look at ways to be happy within the context of our current personal reality.

ORDINARY PEOPLE...

...believe a certain amount of money is the answer for happiness in their lives

...mistake the pursuit of symbols for creating the experience they desire

...translate dissatisfaction to stress and unhappiness

EXTRAORDINARY PEOPLE...

...experience money as an indicator, as feedback and a measurement about their results in life

...focus on what experience they want to create

...accept dissatisfaction as a motivator, a source of creativity, innovation and contribution

~ 29 ~

So, You Want to Be Happy...

Ask most people what they really want in life and they'll tell you, "I just want to be happy." Well, OK, but what does that mean? Before I start discussing happiness, let's take a look at what it does mean, and why so few people seem to be able to find it.

First, happiness is an emotion; it comes and goes, often within the same few minutes. That is why people searching for happiness are doomed to keep on searching: Happiness is momentary, ephemeral, it cannot be relied upon to be there when you decide that that's what you want.

Now joy, that is something altogether different. In spite of circumstances that are bound to give me times of distress and sadness, I can choose the foundation of my life to be one of joy: the joy of being alive. "Happiness" and "joy" are words that are often used interchangeably in casual, everyday speech. In fact, they are two completely different experiences, generated from two distinctly different contexts. It is valuable to understand this distinction, so we can put it into practice in our lives.

I see my life as a part of the earth, a patch of ground to be cultivated. This field I have chosen to call joy. What grows in the field will be some grasses called happiness, and some called anguish, sadness, and disappointment. They are not permanent. They grow, wither and die. And the field of my being remains joyful.

Happiness, however we want to define it, is ephemeral. Sometime we feel happy, sometimes we don't. Will the pursuit of happiness lead to happiness? Look around you and you will see that the answer is a big fat NO. Pursuing happiness is a losing game.

Happiness and the world economy

You already know (don't you?) that money can't buy happiness. You might even have been raised on the old aphorism that, "The best things in life are free." It is probably fair to say that most people believe that to be true. Still, we don't let the truth get in the way of our trying to purchase happiness. We seldom look inside. Our answer to what are essentially internal psychological issues is to look externally, and to increase our material consumption. We go out and buy stuff for every emotional occasion.

If I am depressed or feeling low, I'll try to buy my way out of it with a new outfit, or a new car, a set of golf clubs, a holiday, or dinner and drinks at some expensive place. If I am bored, I'll probably buy even more. When there is something to celebrate, I'll buy flowers, jewelry, champagne or gifts.

Even when I am entering into the process of self-examination, I might believe I can get there solely by spending money on therapy, books, meditation classes or a soul-searching journey to some exotic location.

Quiz time. Try to guess where the following statement came from:

"Money is an article which may be used as a universal passport to everywhere except heaven, and as a universal provider for everything except happiness."

Maybe it came from a church leader, or an ancient Greek philosopher. Perhaps some great oriental guru said it, or was it Julie Andrews in *The Sound of Music*?

Answer: None of the above. It is directly from the daily bulletin of the Temple of Mammon, *The Wall Street Journal*.

Quick! Buy more stuff, or we're all doomed

Success for the global economy is based almost solely upon people buying a lot of "stuff" on a regular basis. When we stop purchasing things—so much of which we don't need—the economy tanks. If people in the United States weren't the biggest consumers of unnecessary goods and services in the world, the global economy would be in real trouble. Every country on earth that needs to sell piles of disposable plastic junk to survive has only to look to the United States to find a market. And now the rest of the world is following in the United States' footsteps. In 1998, when the Japan economy had been in decline for eight years and was getting worse, the Japanese government began issued free coupons for people to buy stuff. Any stuff.

Human beings in the frenetic pursuit of happiness are responsible for a large chunk of the world economy. Trillions and trillions of dollars ever year are spent by hundreds of millions of people in search of ways to be happy. In spite of the fact that we all say, "Money can't buy me love," based on results, many of us believe that money is "The Great Panacea." Then, as soon as we—or a family member or close friend—get seriously ill, we see health as the most important thing. At least until our health returns.

Then, as quick as you can say "S&P 500," back we go to money to solve the ever-elusive problem of happiness.

~ 30 ~

MORE BUCKS OR YEN OR EUROS WILL MAKE IT BETTER, RIGHT?

*He's turned his life around. He used to be depressed
and miserable. Now he's miserable and depressed.*

David Frost

There are a million examples of why more money is not the answer, including well-documented accounts of dozens of big lottery winners whose lives—and the lives of many people around them—have ended in heartbreak. Then there is the sad tale of one of the wealthiest women on the planet, Christina Onassis, who committed suicide at the ripe old age of 35, apparently because she could never be sure whether any of her long list of husbands and boyfriends loved her for herself or her money. I believe that what she really needed is actually free. It can't be bought with any amount of money. It's called self-love.

The idea that money can't buy happiness is such a tired old cliché that we are not really expected to believe it anymore. Yet the notion, or more sophisticated versions of it, has been a key element in practical philosophical thought for centuries.

In today's high-tech world we also have plenty of scientific evidence supporting the view that fame and good looks are no more the answer to happiness and contentment than affluence. An article by Alfie Kohn in the *New York Times* from January 1999, asserts that researchers are amassing an impressive body of data suggesting that satisfaction is simply not for sale.

> "Not only does having more things prove unfulfilling, but people for whom affluence is a priority in life tend to experience an unusual degree of anxiety and depression as well as a lower level of well-being.
>
> Likewise, those who would like nothing more than to be famous or attractive do not fare well, psychologically speaking, as those who primarily want to develop close relationships, become more self-aware, or contribute to the community."

According to Dr. Richard Ryan, professor of psychology at the University of Rochester, and Dr. Tim Kasser, assistant professor of psychology at Knox College in Illinois, the news is even worse.

In three sets of studies published in leading psychological journals since 1993, the researchers sketch an increasingly bleak portrait of people who value "extrinsic goals" like money, fame and beauty. Such people are not only more depressed than others, but also report more behavioral problems and physical discomfort, as well as scoring lower on measures of vitality and self-actualization.

Dr. Ryan and Dr. Kasser said, "...the more we seek satisfaction in material goods, the less we find them there...The fact that pursuing wealth is psychologically unhelpful and often destructive, comes through very strongly in every culture I've looked at. Affluence, per se, does not necessarily result in an unsatisfying life. Problems are primarily associated with living a life where that is your focus."

Another study by the same researchers found that college students who placed great importance on appearance, financial success and popularity were nevertheless rated lower in well-being and self-esteem. Those who aspired to affluence also had more transient relationships, watched more television and were more likely to use cigarettes, alcohol and other drugs than those who placed less emphasis on extrinsic goals.

The article also quotes research from Dr. Aric Rindfleisch at the University of Arizona and Dr. James Burroughs of Rutgers University, who said, "While people who are more materialistic tend to be unhappy with their lives, this effect may be moderated or even eliminated for those who have close, caring relationships."

The truly bad news, according to the Ryan-Kasser work, is that close, caring relationships are often among the casualties of a life devoted to getting rich.

Meanwhile, the madness continues

Despite all this empirical evidence, we continue to spend fortunes on a stupefying array of distractions supposedly designed to make us happier than Liz Taylor at yet another wedding. Cosmetics that contain everything from the placenta of unborn goats to a pound of pig fat mixed with volcanic ash and "19 secret ingredients from the rain forest;" diet products to remove mountains of blubber gained by stuffing ourselves because we are so damn miserable, and miserable because we are so horribly fat; cosmetic surgery in every place from facial to other cheeks; mind-numbing cruises to paradise; luxury boats that never leave their luxury marinas; hard drugs; soft drugs; alcohol; anti-depressants; uppers; downers; frenetic gambling to hit the big time; jewelry that is too expensive to wear; image marriages destined to last all of six months; mink-lined designer toilet seats; lottery tickets; tobacco products we know will kill us; and billions of tons of electronic and plastic and toxic junk that add nothing to our lives and ultimately create only clutter, pollution and landfill.

If any of these external attempts to find happiness actually worked, then we could stop the search. They don't work and yet we never stop the search. Somehow, it only gets worse, more obsessive, more frantic. It is the goal of so many people who come to our seminars: "I just want to find happiness." And that is a big part of the problem. "Find" implies a search outside of ourselves. Happiness is not to be "found" somewhere else.

Soon you'll be happy: Not!

We pursue happiness because we believe it is "out there" somewhere. The fact that nobody on the planet has ever found it "out there" doesn't stop us. "Maybe I'll be the one!" And so the merry chase continues.

A good friend told me once:

> "I can quickly recall how great I felt when I was a student and had nothing at all, and how that happiness didn't seem like enough. At that time, I read Nikos Kazantzakis' wonderful book, *Zorba the Greek,* and felt ecstatic. I was staying, with little money, in the poorest parts of Greece and feeling so happy that I thought it almost unfair. And I think often of that book and that time and how complicated happiness has now become; how much I yearn to reclaim and honor the feelings I had then.
>
> "'How simple and frugal a thing is happiness:,' Kazantzakis reminded me in that book. 'A glass of wine, a roast chestnut, a wretched little brazier, the sound of the sea. All that is required to feel that here and now is happiness is a simple, frugal heart.'"

Happy memories must be left as memories; they can never be reclaimed or relived. In Alan Watts's classic *The Spirit of Zen*, he says,

> "If we suddenly realize that we are happy, the more we endeavor to think of some means of preserving our happiness, the faster we see it slipping away. We try to define happiness so that we may know how to find it when we are feeling miserable; a man thinks, 'I am happy now that I am staying in this place.' And the next time he is unhappy he tries to apply this definition; he goes to that place again and finds that it does not make him happy; there is only the dead memory of happiness, and the definition does not hold."

Henry Miller described happiness in *The Colossus of Maroussi*, another book on the Greek experience:

> "It's good to be plain happy; it's a little better to know that you're happy; but to understand that you're happy and to know why and how and still be happy, be happy in the being and the knowing, well that is beyond happiness, that is bliss."

As much as it might seem that a vacation to a beautiful Greek island will make us happy, the truth is that happiness does not exist in Greece any more or any less than it does in Brisbane or Bangladesh. It does not exist in any *place* at all. Kazantzakis and Miller knew that. My friend says that at the time he did not. He was not alone. Most of us live in a way that suggests that "Greece" is out there somewhere, someday, sometime, and always in that far-off land called The Future.

Anytime but right now, this minute, and in your "simple, frugal heart." "I know that," you say. Sure, you might know it intellectually, but do you really live that way?

The question you need to ask is, is it possible simply to choose to be happy, to get off your "stuff" and wake up? Is that really possible? Here, today, right now? Can you choose to live as though your life may be over in a nanosecond, wring each moment dry and just be happy? Or do you need something to be happy about?

Responsibility · 159

> "Happiness for me is largely a matter of digestion. I have to take cover under an American college president to insure my reputation and respectability when I say that happiness is largely a matter of the movement of the bowels. The American college president in question used to say with great wisdom in his address to each class of freshmen, 'There are only two things I want you to keep in mind: read the Bible and keep your bowels open.' What a wise, genial old soul he was to have said that! If one's bowels move, one is happy, and if they don't move, one is unhappy. That is all there is to it."
>
> Lin Yutang
> The Importance of Living

Let me repeat my point of view: Happiness is emotional, it comes and goes. Joy, on the other hand, is a way of being. It's a choice. I can choose to live my life from a foundation of joy—the joy of being alive. I cannot choose happiness because it is an emotion. Pretending to be happy when I don't really feel that way gives me the plastic smile and the phony enthusiasm of the perennial positive thinking student.

For a little perspective on happiness, maybe you should begin with a good old-fashioned counting of your blessings. You are alive, aren't you? Not a bad place to start. If you need more, think about a little fat book that came out a couple of years back entitled *14,000 Things to be Happy About*. It's just a list. And it could have gone on for another 14,000 things. You don't need a list of 14,000 or 28,000 things. You need a list with only one thing: I choose to be joyful because I am alive.

Is the purpose of life to be happy?

Ask most people what they want in life, and they'll tell you, "To be happy." However, does it work to make happiness the purpose of life? Leo Rosten didn't think so. He said:

> "I cannot believe that the purpose of life is to be 'happy.'
> I think the purpose of life is to be useful, to be responsible,
> to be honorable, to be compassionate. It is, above all, to
> matter: to count, to stand for something, to have made some
> difference that you lived at all."

In my experience with hundreds of thousands of people, I find over and over again that people find meaning and a sense of well-being from living with responsibility, honor and compassion. They see how their lives and their relationships are better served through reaching out and contributing. Happiness, in the sense of being amused, entertained, or getting my personal ego needs met, is pretty insubstantial, unfulfilling fare. With apologies to Thomas Jefferson, it doesn't take long for the "pursuit of happiness" to become boring and stale. If you ask me, there are simply more important things to be done.

Postponing joy

Most people live in what I call "Tomorrowland," a Disney-like village. (I could also call it Fantasyland, and with either title, Disney might sue me.) In our society the emphasis is on tomorrow, next week, next year or the next millennium. The "tomorrow will be better," mindset permeates everything we do. It's that awful "F" word again: the future.

Recently a major investment company ran a worldwide television commercial depicting three young guys who, in 1956, the copy line said, each had $10,000. Two of them went to Europe, had a blast and spent the lot. The other invested his ten grand with Big "F" Financial Enterprises. The two who went to Europe are seen at the end of the commercial, retired and in their sixties, fishing off a pier. Sailing by in his luxury yacht, looking debonair and well pleased with himself, is man number three who (wisely of course) invested with Big F. The final copy line is: "Of course Fred and Joe (on the pier) still have their memories."

In other words, why not do what most people do, and postpone joy? The classic assumption here is that two friends fishing on a pier can't be as joyful as the guy in the yacht. It's another message our culture pounds us with mercilessly: that material wealth equals happiness. It also raises the issue of not sharing your good fortune with your friends, but that's another conversation.

When we can sail past poor old Fred and Joe fishing on the pier, we could be living as though joy were something only for tomorrow. As a result, we never actually achieve the joy we seek, because when the day finally arrives, we'll still be striving to outperform somebody else.

It doesn't get any better than this

One TV commercial did get it right. It was an ad for Old Milwaukee beer. A group of men are sitting around a campfire after a hard day of manly outdoor work, chopping wood and building fences. One guy opens a beer, raises it up and says: "It doesn't get any better than this." Right on. And it's not about the beer. For once, this is wisdom in advertising. It actually doesn't get any better than this, and it won't. Ever. Because right now, this moment, is all we have, and all we will ever have.

Yesterday's gone, and the future doesn't exist, which leaves us with this moment—the here and now—doesn't it?

Well, not if you look at the way most of us sleepwalk through life. If you doubt that most of us run on automatic, take a look around you. Take a little time out to observe the faces of people on the way to work tomorrow. How many do you see who are awake and alert and happy and passionate about being alive? And how many do you see looking downtrodden, morose, more dead than alive while they wait for joy to arrive via the "F" word (that's the Future, remember)? How many do you see sleepwalking, trudging through the day on automatic as their life slips away? More important, are you one of them?

Forget the past and the future; it's easy to see that they don't exist. That kind of leaves the present, right? Well not really. A hundred years ago William James pointed out that we don't even really have that. He said:

> "Let anyone try, I will not say to arrest, but to notice or attend to, the present moment of time. One of the most baffling experiences occurs. Where is it, this present? It has melted in our grasp, fled ere we touch it, gone in the instant of becoming."

Here we are with a past and a future that don't exist, and a present so fleeting it is gone before we can recognize it, and devalued if we do. You'd think that we would therefore appreciate, without reservation, the whatever it is we call the here and the now, to say nothing of the miraculousness of our very being. Instead, we devote ourselves to complaints about stuff like restaurant service, our spouse leaving the toilet seat up or down and the weather.

The receptionist with one of our corporate clients put me straight on complaining many years ago. I came into her office wringing wet one morning, moaning about the wind and rain as I passed by her desk. I felt miserable. She looked disgustingly happy as she responded to my nonsense. "Hey, Mr. White," she called out as I dripped sullenly across the hallway, "you woke up this morning, didn't you? You're still breathing, aren't you? Well so am I. Wow, I think this is great weather!" That is real enlightenment.

Our lives, along with the weather and happiness, will forever be up and down and sideways and all over the place. That's how life and the weather are, and that is as good as it gets. How do I know that? Simple. It is all I've got. If the future does not exist and the past is gone, then this must be as good as it gets, because there is, right now, nothing else. And even if you don't believe the truth of that statement, living each moment as if now is absolutely as good as it gets will have you celebrating your life every day. Not a bad way to live. In fact, it might even be described as extraordinary.

ORDINARY PEOPLE...

...focus on happiness as a goal

...believe money will somehow make them happy

...postpone opportunities for joy till "someday"

EXTRAORDINARY PEOPLE...

...recognize happiness as just another emotional state—it will come and go

...acknowledge that true joy can be present in simply living our lives

...create an extraordinary relationship with the money they have—no matter how much or how little

...realize it doesn't get any better than this, this is it, this is the only life we have

~ 31 ~

THE GREATEST LOVE OF ALL

Of all the judgments we pass in life, none is as important as the one we pass on ourselves.

Dr. Nathaniel Branden
The Six Pillars of Self Esteem

Internationally recognized expert on self-esteem Dr. Nathaniel Branden says that to face life with low self-esteem is to be at a severe disadvantage and self-love is essential to building self- esteem. He asserts that "the love we have for our own life…is the beginning of virtue. It is the launching pad for our noblest aspirations. It is the motive power that drives the six pillars. It is the seventh pillar of self-esteem."

> "Because the greatest love of all is happening to me
> I've found the greatest love of all inside of me
> The greatest love of all is easy to achieve
> Learning to love yourself, it is the greatest love of all"
>
> "Greatest Love of All"
> Performed by Whitney Houston
> Written by Linda Creed and
> Michael Masser

What a great song. It speaks to the heart, and deeply. It powerfully affirms the human spirit, the quest for self-love and self-esteem, the pride in being alive that each of us is entitled to experience simply by being born a human being.

It's a common misconception that there is something narcissistic, boastful and wrong in loving one's self. The assumption is that you are trying to impress others, to get them to love you. In fact, the opposite is true. True self-love is not about trying to get others to love you. If you really have self-love, you are not hungrily searching for the acceptance of others; you welcome it, but you don't need it.

There is thus a big difference between honoring ourselves as important (self-love) and doing things to make ourselves look good in the eyes of others.

In fact, building up an "image" by piling up money or driving the right car or having the right friends is often a sign that I *lack* self-love. Again, Dr. Branden:

> "Nothing is more common than to pursue self-esteem by means that cannot and will not work. Instead of seeking it through consciousness, responsibility, and integrity, we may seek it through popularity, material acquisitions, or sexual exploits. Instead of valuing personal authenticity, we may value belonging to the right clubs, or the right church, or the right political parties."

Of course, it doesn't work. If I feel empty inside because I believe that I'm inferior and unlovable, no amount of external popularity or possessions or sexual conquests will fill that void. Until I experience that I am valuable and lovable for who I am, not for what I have or what I can do, I will continue to look for self-love in all the wrong places.

Are you throwing away your birthright?

Self-love is our natural state. If life's trials and tribulations have caused you to become cynical about this, go spend a half-hour around a normal, healthy two-year-old. You and I were once this way: bright, energetic, powerful, trusting, loving, full of laughter and joy, overflowing with self-love.

No small child ever came into the world feeling inferior, filled up with self-loathing and self-doubt. It took a lot of painful experiences, a lot of scolding and criticism and other forms of disapproval, to turn that beautiful child into an adult who can't stand to look at his face in the mirror. The belief that I'm not as good as other people, that the real me is unlovable, is the most common limiting belief in the world. It's what we're being right about when we sabotage our success, when we punish ourselves, when we feel undeserving. It's why we build up an image to hide ourselves behind, and why we wear around a thick layer of emotional armor to keep ourselves from being hurt.

That's the bad news. The good news is that your self-love hasn't died. You didn't outgrow it or lose it along the way. It's still there within you, waiting to be tapped, waiting to be released. It may be deeply buried and well-hidden—

even from yourself. Our experience with hundreds of thousands of people shows that rediscovering a deep and lasting self-love is possible for all of us.

There are dozens of reasons to justify loving yourself and you don't need "logical" reasons. You were born one hundred percent full of self-love. It is the human animal's natural state of being. Not to love yourself is unnatural. It takes conscious effort. To return to your natural state is a challenging and critical project. You must examine the self-limiting beliefs you have created. You must acknowledge the ways you have sold yourself short, settling for less than your truest aspirations. You will need to clear away the dead wood of denying who you really are, of living your life for survival instead of self-expression, so that you can see the real you again. And in seeing who you really are, you can discover the greatest gift of all—yourself.

ORDINARY PEOPLE...

...seek self esteem through the approval of others

...accept limiting beliefs and judgments that deny self-acceptance and self-love

EXTRAORDINARY PEOPLE...

...fully realize the gift they are and through self-love, gain all the approval they'll ever need—their own

...know that they are loved, guided and protected

~ 32 ~

WHAT YOU RESIST, PERSISTS

*The skilled master of life never opposes things; he never tries to change
things by asserting himself against them; he yields to their full force...without
ever encountering their direct opposition. That is to say, he treats them
positively; he changes them by acceptance,
by taking them into his confidence, never by flat denial.*
Allan Watts
The Spirit of Zen

What you resist persists. It might sound illogical and counter-intuitive. If I want to get rid of something, I should oppose it, overcome it, conquer it, right? Well, maybe not. A couple of examples:

An articulate 32-year-old man (I'll call him Gustavo) attended one of our seminars in Hong Kong. His father, a former soccer star and extremely successful banker, was well known and highly respected in their native country, Brazil. Despite his family's pleading to stay in Brazil and work in his father's bank, Gustavo had moved with his wife and two young children to a small apartment in Hong Kong. Almost weekly, he got requests from his family to return to his native country. Although he had a good relationship with his father, at least on the surface, Gustavo adamantly refused to go back.

"I don't want to just follow in my father's footsteps," he said. "I want to be myself, and make it on my own."

In spite of the fact that he loved his father, Gustavo moved all the way to Hong Kong to try to get away from his influence. He said he wanted to be different from his father, to find himself, to be his own man. A concurrent reality was that instead of focusing on developing his own unique skills and talents, Gustavo was constantly attempting not to be like his father. He was always comparing himself to his dad, always competing in obvious and not-so-obvious ways with his father's athletic prowess and his business success. In fact, Gustavo's entire life was lived in resistance.

He was an excellent tennis player, but he got little enjoyment out of the sport, because he constantly criticized himself for not being good enough to make it at the top professional level. He was a successful tennis coach in Hong

Kong, but because of his need to prove himself, because of his resistance to his father, he was trapped. He wasn't truly free to explore his own interests or his own unique gifts.

Gustavo didn't particularly want to be in Hong Kong. He longed to be back in his home country. But wouldn't allow himself to go back until, as he said, "I make it on my own." Keeping so much distance between himself and his family was another way for Gustavo to resist his father's control—to do the opposite of what his father wanted him to do. And as long as he continued to resist his father, Gustavo could never to return to Brazil—no matter how much he dreamed of returning.

Gustavo was stuck with what he resisted, in a go-nowhere cycle. He resisted being inferior to his father, so he always felt inadequate. As Gustavo and I talked about it in the seminar, it became clear to him that until he let go of his need to prove he was as good as his father, he would continue to feel trapped and boxed in. Until he became OK with himself as a unique human being, and learned to love himself as he really was, he would be doomed always to come up short.

I remember saying to him, "Gustavo, it must be exhausting to carry around all this resistance to your father 24 hours a day. Are you ready to let him go, to let him be himself, and allow Gustavo to be who he really is?"

"I think I am," he said. "I realized today that my father's not going to live forever. I don't want him to die with me so far away."

"Some of us, and I was one of those people for a long time, go on resisting our Dads even after they're dead," I said. "You're lucky. You still have the chance to break this pattern before it's too late."

To live in resistance to someone is to give them your power. Gustavo came to understand that; not just intellectually, but from the heart, where it matters. He understood that by staying in resistance, nothing would change, even after his Dad was dead and gone.

Being in resistance 24 hours a day is demanding and exhausting work. In resistance, nothing flows or can ever be easy and simple. Resistance implies friction, and the burning up of energy. When you push the brake pedal on your car, the brake linings impose huge resistance on the brake drum, causing the car to stop. The energy required to make the car stop is enormous; so is the energy needed to live in resistance and the result is much the same: It impedes our forward motion, it blocks us from the experience of an extraordinary life.

Resistance can translate to revenge

The resistance that comes from anger and hatred is even more disabling than that evoked by envy and self-doubt, such as Gustavo's. A woman in one of our seminars (I'll call her Annie) harbored anger for her Father that went back thirty years. When Annie was 12, her Father had left her Mother for another woman. Heartbroken, her Mother had become bedridden, an invalid, and died when Annie was 18. Thirty years after her Father had walked out Annie still hated him.

Like everyone who hangs onto anger or hatred, Annie felt as though she was exacting revenge; that her anger somehow made her Father pay for what he'd done. In truth, her Father controlled her life even though he had lived thousands of miles away. Her day-to-day experience was dominated by the anger and hatred she'd built up over the years, and it was Annie herself who was paying the price. Since she took out her rage at her Father on all the men in her life, her romantic relationships never lasted more than a few months. Even though she very much wanted to have a child, at the age of 42 she'd never been married.

Like many of us, Annie continued to act out her anger in reaction to events that had happened years before. Her memory of her Dad held all the power in her life, but in her need to be right, she could not see that. For his part, her distancing herself from him upset him at first, but as there seemed to be nothing he could do about it he chose to get on with his life. Annie's anger and hostile behavior persisted for 30 years. Then, her Father died.

Maybe she assumed that her anger would die with him. It didn't. In fact, it seemed to get worse. She came to one of our seminars, realizing that she needed to find a way to forgive, or her memory of her Father would continue to control her life.

Annie was finally able to forgive her Father with the help of a simple but powerful idea: *Her dad had done the best job he was capable of doing.* If he had known a way to be a better Father, he would have been one. There are few schools to teach people how to be good parents. How each of us raises our children is usually based on the way we were raised by our parents or in reaction to the way we were raised, and the times in which we live. Each of us does the best job we can do with our children.

The moment when Annie understood that as long as she continued to resist her Father, all the unhappiness of broken and troubled relationships with men would persist. It was as though a mountain had been lifted off her slender shoulders.

In my experience, all of us are in resistance somewhere in our lives. We can choose to convert our resistance and use it to our advantage. By looking closely at what you resist, you have the opportunity to gain valuable insights, to learn and to grow. In fact, resistance can be a valuable tool if you are willing to stop and notice it. When someone makes a suggestion at work or in your family, do you automatically resist? Do you have an identifiable pattern of resisting men or women, people in authority, people who are weak or needy? Do you resist wealthy or otherwise successful people?

The awareness gained from answering such questions can push you to stop and ask "what's that about?" Where and when and how was that resistance created? At that point there is often much to be discovered, learned and resolved. The result is always the freeing up of your energy, a movement from contraction and feeling heavy to one of expanding and feeling lighter. If you don't deal with resistance, you remain stuck. It never goes away on its own, it just gets tougher to deal with.

Whaddayyawant?

OK, so what *do* you want? That, after all, is the big question. The "Who am I?" question is fine. Then what? Beyond a certain point it leads nowhere and is unsatisfying. It is where we are headed that is important to us. A great forward step in life is to focus a serious personal inquiry on our direction and fulfillment, it's about answering the question: "What do you want?"

Well...*what do you want?*

This is a question that can assist you to dig deep down inside yourself. Life sometimes asks the question impolitely, but then life is sometimes not polite. Life is right in your face, often screaming at you in frustration, sometimes complicated and confusing, always changing. And from time to time it will step up and whack you impolitely over the head with the unexpected.

Here's my point of view: At some level, each one of us knows exactly what we want. I do, and so do you. You simply have to be willing to reach inside and discover what's really there. If you run away, if you're unwilling to face yourself and uncover the truth, you'll remain confused, because confusion is one of the best ways available to avoid seeing the truth. Still, you do know what you want. We all do.

By the way, in our experience with more than 500,000 participants in our seminars, the answer to what you want is not a new Ferrari or a digital watch that can program your VCR from 200 feet underwater off some Caribbean island. You don't even want a new relationship—except a new relationship with yourself.

The answer to what we all want is not those "things" outside ourselves. What we want are vivid experiences within: the experience of freedom, joy, aliveness, peace of mind, security, love, self confidence and self esteem (the list goes on—add the ones that are important to you).

Things outside of ourselves—including money, relationships, children, career, all of them—are not ends in themselves. They are all mechanisms, means through which we can create what we really want. And what stops us from being able to have the experiences we want, from moment to moment? Once again, it's our limiting beliefs: "I don't deserve love." "I'm not smart enough to make big money." "I'm not capable of real success." Just as what we really want is not outside ourselves, what prevents us from having what we want is not outside ourselves, either.

It's all within.

So, what do you want? Well, take a look at what you've got. Whatever it is, whether you like it or not, it's not there by accident. You got what you have through the beliefs you hold, the choices you made and the actions you took. You may say you don't have what you want, however—based on results—you have what's "right" for you. Meaning that you have what's consistent with your beliefs about yourself, other people, and the world. How could it be otherwise?

And if you don't like what you have in your life, the message is simple. Wake up! You have beliefs that you're not aware of, and those beliefs are causing you to make choices and take actions that are not in your best interest. What you have at this moment is just a mirror of your belief system. By becoming more aware, and by living your life from the responsible point of view, you can begin to have the experience of life that you really want.

ORDINARY PEOPLE...

...live in reaction to past events and people

...live in resistance and continue to create resistance in themselves and others

...deny or avoid knowing what they really want and often substitute symbols like houses or cars or trophy relationships

EXTRAORDINARY PEOPLE...

...learn from the past and let it go

...learn from what they resist and let it go

...learn and act to achieve the experience they really want to create... like freedom, joy and love

~ Part 4 ~

COMMUNICATION
*Why awareness and responsibility
are useless without it*

~ 33 ~

A Soaring Eagle, or a Jabbering Parrot?

*Most conversations are simply monologues
delivered in the presence of a witness.*

Margaret Millar

It doesn't matter how aware or responsible you are; in today's complex and interconnected world, you can achieve very little on your own. That means you will need to enroll the people in your life—your family or friends or colleagues—in your vision and your dreams, gain their support and overcome their objections. All of which requires that you be able to successfully articulate your wants, needs and requests for action. This is effective communication. As Sir Winston Churchill, a masterful communicator, so eloquently put it, "When the eagles are silent, the parrots begin to jabber." In other words, if I want to soar, I need to positively declare my goals and dreams and shape the conversation around me. Only then will I begin to shape my own life. If I don't, then others will shape it for me and I probably won't like how my life turns out.

Believe it or not, you are always totally committed. The question is—to what?

Some years ago, I watched the painful television spectacle of the Californian triathlete, Julie Moss, in the finishing stages of the most grueling race on earth, the Ironman Triathlon in Hawaii. She was one of the favorites to win the women's event. After more than ten hours of non-stop swimming, bike riding and running, she was about a mile in the lead, and with less than a mile left to run. At that point she hit the wall, and began staggering and sometimes crawling along the road towards the finish line, dehydrated, cramped, disoriented and completely spent. Soon, her closest friend, another Californian, ran past her to win this major event.

When the race was over, a TV reporter asked her how she felt. Her astonishing reply was, "A little tired."

The reporter said, "No, I mean how do you feel about losing the race?"

Moss replied, "I was committed, but only to finishing. I wasn't committed to winning. If I had been committed to winning, I would have won it."

The next year, she did win it.

What are you committed to?

There is a huge lesson here: We are always committed to *something*. However, we're not always committed to what we say we're committed to—or even to what we think we're committed to. Suppose you're watching TV and I ask you to run to the corner store and back. If you say, "OK, I'm on it," yet you remain crashed out in front of the TV, you're not being lazy; you're committed. Not to running to the store—you're committed to watching TV.

In other words, there is only one way to measure commitment. Look at the results. You can always tell what you—or anyone else—are committed to, based on the results you have produced.

I find that people who measure their commitments by simply looking at their results are people who experience enormous freedom. They no longer carry around the burden of guilt or failure that comes about when we say we're committed to one thing, but our results tell a different story. People who live their lives "based on results" are dealing with the reality of "what is" as opposed to wishful thinking.

This doesn't mean we have a duty to remain committed to something when it is clearly not in our best interests. If I make a commitment to a job, but my boss demands that I work nights and weekends without any overtime pay or compensatory time off, and constantly finds fault and criticizes me in a way that is unfair and abusive, I am not obligated to stick it out just because I made a commitment. In fact, if I let myself be abused over and over again, what I am actually committed to (probably unconsciously) is being abused. If I am truly committed to my own well-being, as well as the well-being of others, I will remove myself from situations in which other people are trying to use me or take advantage of me. Staying in a situation which is bad for me, under the pretense of honoring my commitment, is often a disguised form of unworthiness, an acting out of a belief that sounds something like: "I deserve to suffer."

This is not to say that hanging in there when the going is rough is never the right thing to do. Sometimes it's exactly what you need to do to create the results you want. What makes the difference is clarity regarding the question: "What am I committed to?" When you're clear and grounded about what you're really committed to, you'll know what actions need to be taken.

We are always committed to something. Some people are even committed to being uncommitted. They say things like, "In my relationship, I'm just hanging around to see how it goes. Perhaps we have a future together, perhaps not." Or, wouldn't you love to be working with someone who says, "This job is OK for now—I like the paycheck. It's not what I really want but it will do for now."

One hundred percent is easy; ninety-nine is tough

"Commitment" is a word we use in everyday conversation to mean a lot of different things. In the strict sense of the word, a "commitment" is unconditional. Real commitment means one hundred percent. In losing that race so dramatically, and in winning it easily the following year, Julie Moss gave the world a clear example of the difference between what we say we're committed to compared to what our true commitment is. She also provided a dramatic illustration of the difference between 100 percent commitment to something and 99 percent. Simply put, 100 percent is easy; 99's is very difficult and never works to accomplish what we really want.

Imagine how difficult a job is when you are not quite focused, compared to when you are really focused and on fire with enthusiasm. Notice how the time flies when you are totally involved, fully committed. Think of how easy it seems. If you are a little bit distracted, or not totally involved, it's tough. It seems to take forever, and you seldom get the results that you want. Athletes know the distinction between these two states of being only too well. It's called being "in the zone." In this state everything seems effortless—and the results, like the commitment, are 100 percent.

In fact, total commitment gets us more than 100 percent.

Leader of The Scottish Himalayan expedition, W.H. Murray, knew that better than anyone. His now famous statement on the subject is a masterpiece, and well worth quoting in full:

"Until one is committed, there is hesitancy, the chance to draw back, always ineffectiveness. Concerning all acts of initiative (and creation) there is one elementary truth, the ignorance of which kills countless ideas and splendid plans: That the moment one definitely commits oneself, then Providence moves too. All sorts of things occur to help one that would never otherwise have occurred. A whole stream of events issues from the decision, raising in one's favor all manner of unforeseen incidents and meetings and material assistance, which no man could have dreamed would have come his way. I have learned a deep respect for one of Goethe's couplets: 'Whatever you can do, or dream you can, begin it. Boldness has genius, power and magic in it.'"

You can avoid and deny and find reasons and excuses. You can play victim and blame circumstances or other people or fate. The reality is that when you fail to achieve the results you want, it is because you weren't 100 percent committed. Or, more accurately, you were committed to something different than what you told everybody—and yourself—that you were committed to. It's a cop out, just another excuse for not accomplishing your goal, when you know deep down you weren't committed enough to make it happen.

When you set yourself an achievable goal, remember you are either committed to it or you're not. Similarly, you can't be just a little bit pregnant.

You buy my bull*#%?... and I'll buy yours

Our culture has convinced us that honesty in our personal relationships is definitely not the best policy. We tell others what we think they want to hear, or what we believe is good for them, or a version of the truth that we imagine will not hurt their feelings—anything to avoid the embarrassment of confrontation. It's called, and pardon the rough language, "You buy my bullshit, I'll buy yours." We do it every day with stuff like, "Hey, great to see you again (name forgotten), let's get together and catch up." "Great. Let's get in touch. I'll give you a call."

Following the maxim that most great humor is grounded in truth, here's what a wag called "Four Levels of Beverly Hills Insincerity" and usually delivered over the shoulder on parting:

1. "I'll call you."
2. "I'll call you. Let's do lunch."
3. "I'll call you. Let's do lunch. Love ya baby."
4. "I'll call you. Let's do lunch. Love ya baby."
 (long pause) "Mean it!"

Of course, these people have no intention of contacting the other, but they're both masterful at pretending intimacy and buying each other's lies. We imagine it to be harmless, and in some situations perhaps it is.

Then again, imagine what the academic world would be like if your teachers and professors always marked your papers with high scores so as not to hurt your feelings, or because they thought it would make you happy (unfortunately, this is actually happening!). It might make you happy for a short time, but you wouldn't receive much of an education. If you are serious about learning, you want to know where you are on track and where you're off, and that requires honest feedback from your mentors.

The same is true in life. It does not serve my best interests if the people closest to me keep telling me only what I want to hear. What if your doctor told you that you were perfectly well, when you had a life-threatening disease? Or if your accountant painted a rosy picture for you when you were in fact almost bankrupt?

We often say we can't be honest with our friends or colleagues, or even with our wife or husband, our parents, our brothers and sisters, because we're afraid we may hurt their feelings. We convince ourselves that we withhold what we really think or feel out of consideration for the other person. In reality, however, the person we're actually protecting in not being honest is ourselves. Our real motive for not speaking the truth is usually to avoid anger or disapproval from someone else. We don't want to risk being rejected, so it's easier to lie, or just not to say anything.

At another level, of course, you and I have no power whatsoever to hurt anybody else's feelings. If I tell you that your new haircut makes you look unattractive, you can choose to feel offended, to laugh and think I have no sense of what's in style, or to appreciate my feedback as valuable information. What I communicate about you is not in and of itself either hurtful or helpful. You get to decide how to receive it. Feedback is simply information. How you choose to respond to it is up to you.

This is true even when someone's intention in giving feedback is to damage you. If I call you a liar and a cheat, trying to get you to feel bad, you still have a choice about how to react. And if you "get your feelings hurt," chances are it's because you secretly suspect that you're a liar and a cheat. If you're secure in the knowledge that you're an honest, upright person, my calling you a liar and a cheat won't be upsetting. Whether or not you get your feelings hurt, in other words, is once again up to you.

Fearless feedback is fabulous

Here's a wonderful example of what I mean by honest and valuable feedback. I came across the following in the January, 1999 edition of *Harper's Magazine*. These are letters exchanged by Joseph P. Kennedy, father of U.S. President John F. Kennedy, and Harold Laski, in August 1940. At the time, the senior Kennedy was the U.S. Ambassador to Great Britain and Laski was a professor at London School of Economics. Earlier that summer, John F. Kennedy had graduated from Harvard and had arranged for his senior thesis to be published as *While England Slept*.

Dear Harold,

I have just received two copies of Jack's book by air mail from the States. I thought you would be interested in reading it. I gave one to the Prime Minister, and as this is the only one I have, I should appreciate your sending it back to me as soon as you have finished it. The reviews have been swell...If you feel like writing him a line, I know he would be delighted to hear from you.

Sincerely, Joe Kennedy

Dear Joe,

The easy thing for me to do would be to repeat the eulogies that Krock and Harry Luce have showered on your boy's work.

In fact, I choose the more difficult way of regretting deeply that you let him publish it. For while it is the book of a lad with brains, it is very immature, it has no real structure, and it dwells almost wholly on the surface of things. In a good university, half a hundred seniors do books like this as part of their normal work in their final year. But they don't publish them for the good reason that their importance lies in what they get out of doing them, not what they have to say.

I don't honestly think any publisher would have looked at that book of Jack's if he had not been your son, and if you had not been Ambassador. And those are not the right grounds for publication.

I care a lot about your boys. I don't want them to be spoilt as rich men's sons are so easily spoilt. Thinking is a hard business, and you have to pay the price for admission to it. Do believe that these hard sayings from me represent much more real friendship than the easy praise of "yes men" like Arthur Krock.

Yours very sincerely, Harold J. Laski

Wow! That's a "fabulous" example of "fearless feedback!"

As I pointed out earlier, just as an airplane heading from New York to Rome requires constant course corrections to keep from being diverted by the forces of wind and gravity, course corrections are required in our lives also. To keep the plane from ending up in Athens requires regular adjustments in direction, altitude and speed—which are made on the basis of feedback obtained regularly from the plane's computers. If the feedback is ignored, the passengers and crew are in deep manure. Feedback in our lives is no different.

In order to get where you want to go—in fact, even to know where you are actually starting from—you need feedback from other people who care about how you are doing in life. I like Werner Erhard's idea about the need to have "committed listeners" in our lives, people who have both the ability to truly hear us when we speak about our lives and a knowledge of our purpose, our values and our vision. Only then can these friends call us on our "stuff", our reasons, stories, excuses and ways we avoid. Only then can they truly serve us with actionable feedback.

What's your word really worth?

We are only as good as our word.
Dennis Becker

It was evening three during an Extraordinary Living Seminar of about 150 students. Although he had agreed at the beginning of the seminar (like everyone else) to be in his seat on time, one middle-aged man had consistently arrived late. And tonight, he was late again. He came into the room, found a chair, and sat down. Here was an opportunity for him—and everybody in the seminar—to learn a valuable lesson. I stopped my interaction with the group and asked the man (I'll call him Jason) to stand.

"Jason," I said, "do you acknowledge that you have a broken agreement?"

"What agreement," he asked.

"Two days ago, you stood up with the rest of the group and agreed to be on time," I said. "Remember?"

"OK, so I'm late," he said. "So what? Why do you want to make such a big deal out of it?"

"Because it is a big deal," I replied. "I don't mean being late. That's not a big deal. I mean the fact that you made an agreement with me and everybody else in here—and with yourself—to be on time, and you've consistently broken that agreement. That is a big deal."

Jason, a highly successful businessman, looked at me like I was crazy. Then his eyes wandered around the room in search of support, as if to say to his fellow students, "Hey, help me out here, this guy is nuts." They returned his unspoken pleas with blank looks—perhaps seeing themselves in his "story."

"So, Jason," I said, "are you willing to see if there's something for you to learn about yourself here?"

He shrugged his shoulders. "I guess so," he said.

"Is that a 'yes' or a 'no?'" I asked.

"Yes," he said.

"OK," I said. "Then tell me, what was your intention in being late?"

"Look, Robert," he said with a melodramatic sigh, "I'm very busy at work. I intended to be here on time, but I stopped at the office this morning and was on a long distance call that lasted longer than I thought it would, and then I got stuck in traffic. So I'm late, OK?"

"I understand that you've got some good reasons for being late," I said. "And as we've been saying, the only way to tell what your real intentions are is to look at the results. So, based on results, what does it look like your intention was in this situation?"

"I told you," he said, "my intention was to be on time. But things happen, like important phone calls and traffic jams. It was just impossible for me to get here on time."

"Well, let's take a look," I said. "I understand that your work is important to you. Given that, was it impossible for you to keep your agreement?"

"OK," he said, "I guess it would have been possible for me to be here on time. But I would have had to hang up on my most important customer right in the middle of a negotiation that's going to be worth more than a million dollars to my company."

"Right," I said. "So, based on results, what was more important to you than keeping your agreement to be on time to the seminar?"

"What was more important?" he said. "My business. My company. Making sure I don't lose that customer."

"Exactly," I said. "If this seminar was more important to you, you would have kept your agreement and been here on time. You'd have made sure you left your office with enough time to get here. Based on results, what's important to you is your business. And when push comes to shove, you'll break the promises you make with people in your life when those promises conflict with your business. Your work takes precedence, right?"

He nodded his head, so I continued. "So, tell me Jason, how is this a reflection of the way you live your life?"

"I don't know what you mean," he said.

"Well, who's an important person in your life—other than yourself?"

"My 10-year-old daughter," he said.

"In what ways do you treat your daughter just like you treated us in the seminar tonight? How often do you make promises to her—and then break them because your business comes first?"

"What makes you think I don't keep my promises to my daughter?"

"Because you haven't kept your promise to me and your fellow students. You break your agreements with us consistently and think nothing of it. So, I'd ask you to look for a minute at the promises you break with your daughter. Think about it. How many times have you told her you'd attend a school event, and instead stayed at the office? Or said you'd be back in time for dinner, and arrived home when she was in bed asleep?"

Jason's defiant mood suddenly changed. His head went down. Staring quietly at the floor, this Captain of Industry began to cry.

"Jason," I said, "this is why we're all here. To find out what matters to us—and where we're out of touch with ourselves. And right now you and your example are our teachers."

The prices you pay for broken promises

How many people do you know who consistently show up late for lunch or a meeting or whatever? How often do you show up late, even by a few minutes? A simple meeting for coffee and you're ten minutes late (as usual). You give your usual feeble and mostly phony excuses, blaming the traffic or a meeting you couldn't get out of, while the person you kept waiting nods approvingly that it's OK.

Unfortunately, it's not OK—and deep down both of you know it.

There are prices to pay for those broken agreements, prices for you and prices for others. Every time you break an agreement you lose self-esteem, self-respect and self-confidence, and, you lose other people's trust in you as well. Every time you keep an agreement you increase these same valuable assets, accordingly. It is just the way things are.

AGREEMENTS

Prices for breaking	Rewards for keeping
Lose trust from others	Gain trust from others
Destroy relationships	Build relationships
Lower self confidence	Increase confidence
Damage self esteem	Raise self esteem
Undermine self respect	Enhance self respect
Confusion, loss of clarity	More clarity, focus
Lower energy level	Higher energy level

Contrary to what many people think, there is no such thing as an unimportant broken agreement. There may be bigger external consequences for breaking some agreements than others—but there are no broken agreements without a price. If you break your agreement to drive at or below the speed limit, and you hit another car and kill someone, the external consequences will be big. If you tell your daughter you're coming to her soccer game and then don't show up, even though there are no apparent external consequences, you still pay an automatic price. You've inevitably lost some of your daughter's trust in you, you've damaged her self esteem and your own, you've undermined the respect she has for you as a parent, and your relationship is a little less close. Break your agreements with your daughter enough times and you'll lose your relationship with her entirely. Broken agreements destroy trust and the outcome is often damaged or even destroyed marriages, friendships, and relationships with colleagues.

Tragedy: Your cup no longer runneth over

In that seminar with Jason, I told the group that to understand the effect that broken agreements have on us, we can use the metaphor of an approval cup. When you're born, your approval cup is full to overflowing with self-approval; you have all the self-worth you'll ever need. However, as we grow up, many of us are criticized and made wrong over and over by our parents, teachers, other adults, and even our friends. When this happens, our approval cup begins to leak. Every time you are told that you're not good enough, or you're a bad boy or girl, or you've done it wrong again, it knocks another hole in your approval cup. By the time you reach adolescence, your cup feels empty, because your self worth has pretty much leaked out. And what knocks more holes in your approval cup than anything else? Broken agreements. Broken promises. Not keeping your word. Or having somebody you care about make a promise to you that they don't keep.

Then, tragedy: When your approval cup gets empty, you look for approval, for your sense of self-esteem and self worth, outside of yourself. It's automatic. Of course, there's a major problem with this formula: Nobody else's approval can ever fill you up or sustain your needs. And if your sense of self worth and self confidence comes from somebody else's approval, when that person doesn't approve of you any more, self esteem drains away and your cup is empty again. As long as you look outside of yourself for approval, you can never be fulfilled—and here we're defining fulfilled as meaning filled full of self worth.

Broken agreements hurt. Every time Jason didn't make it home to play with his daughter, she went to bed in pain. And what do you think she decided about herself? The same thing you or I or anybody would decide: that she must not be worth very much if her own father couldn't be bothered to be there with her when he said he would. Her self-worth suffered, and so did Jason's. Broken agreements are a lose/lose game. Nobody wins; everybody suffers.

Breaking agreements with others is bad enough. Breaking agreements with yourself can be even more damaging. Since agreements with yourself are often private promises that only you know about, they are that much easier to break. Hey, make an agreement with yourself to lose weight or stop smoking or get up early and exercise and you can break it any old time. Nobody knows. Well, not quite nobody. You know. And you have to live with yourself 24 hours a day.

If you are an obsessive/compulsive agreement keeper, does that mean your life will work infinitely better? No, it won't. What keeping your agreements can do is clear the fog of confusion that broken agreements creates, and allow you to see more clearly what's working in your life, and what is not. I believe that keeping your agreements with yourself and other people is a positive way to live. And remember: There is no universal law on agreement keeping. So don't get angry and upset and become a victim when you keep your agreements and other people didn't keep theirs.

It simply works when you deliver work on the date you promised it, keep your marriage or relationship agreements and otherwise match your behavior to your promises.

When you get right down to it in relationships with your self and others, your word is all you've got. Beyond your word there is nothing; no basis for trust and no foundation for self-worth. Keep your word and you enjoy the trust and respect of others. And you'll find the automatic by-product is that you trust and respect yourself more and more every day.

Ordinary People...

...are casual about broken agreements

...are unconscious about the effects of broken agreements, the erosion of trust and damage to their relationships

Extraordinary People...

...make fewer agreements and keep the ones they make

...in the rare event of a broken agreement, they "clean it up" with all concerned

...stay conscious about their agreements and the role of agreements in constantly building trust in all relationships

~ 34 ~

BE SELFISH:
GIVE, GIVE, GIVE—THEN GIVE SOME MORE

*The Sea of Galilee and the Dead Sea are made from the
same water. It flows down, clear and cool, from the heights
of Hebron and the roots of the cedars of Lebanon.
The Sea of Galilee makes beauty of it, for the Sea of Galilee
has an outlet. It gets to give. It gathers its riches that it may pour
them out again to fertilize the Jordan plain. The Dead Sea with
the same water makes horror. For the Dead sea has no outlet.
It gets to keep.*

Henry Emerson Fosdick
The Meaning of Service

Of the many thousands of people who have completed our more advanced personal effectiveness program, The Breakthrough Experience, ninety-nine percent of them will be bouncing off the walls with excitement. Ask them why, and you'll get many different answers. In truth, all the answers are just differing forms of a single underlying answer: "I've just spent 40 intensive hours giving of myself to others." Our discovery is that a high percentage of the petty neurosis that plague citizens of the developed world "clear up" the moment people get outside their self-involvement and simply give to others.

"Awareness" is the central theme and focus of The Breakthrough Experience yet giving of oneself is the vehicle for participation, learning and success. We've designed these four intensive days so that in numerous ways, participants have a direct experience of giving of themselves. They experience this giving deeply, although they may not be able to immediately articulate exactly what it was they were doing. When a participant shares a story from his or her life with emotional honesty, that is an act of giving to others. And in many other ways—being honest, participating fully and spontaneously, showing up authentically—students are able to give to one another.

Of course, it is not only in our seminars that giving of oneself to others is a powerfully fulfilling experience. Well documented findings of the last few thousand years of human civilization prove that the most direct and satisfying way to be enriched and rewarded in life is to give. And, contrary to some people's beliefs, giving is also the most direct way to get what you want. I'm sure you've heard dozens of philosophical statements supporting this view. Here's one from Jeffrey Moses:

"The giving of money, time, support and encouragement to worthy causes can never be detrimental to the giver. The laws of nature are structured so that acts of charity will open an individual to an unbounded reservoir of riches."

Giving and receiving are two sides of the same coin. To take from people and from life, without giving in return, is an empty, shallow and unrewarding experience. When we give, we automatically receive. We have the privilege of feeling good about the gift, and about who we are as a giver. In my direct personal experience, most people discover that true joy is sourced in treating life not as a place to get things, but as a place to give oneself to others.

As a small child, perhaps you preferred to receive Christmas and birthday gifts rather than to give them. As an adult, I am willing to bet you would rather experience the joy of thinking about, buying and giving a gift, than receiving one. Why stop there? Why not give of yourself all the time, and feel the richness of giving all the time? Why do we hold back from giving? It is, after all, our natural state. We are born to give.

Human beings have an infinite capacity for two things: giving and love. Do you think Mother Teresa ever ran out of love and care to give to the sick and the destitute? At nearly 85 years of age, and with a weak heart, she was still out there giving; traveling and speaking, caring and working as she had been every day since she was a novice. That's because giving nourishes and replenishes the giver. Taking depletes us and burns us out.

Are you a giver or a taker?

Look at the life of the thousands of everyday heroes in your community and you know that there are givers in the world, people who in most every situation ask: "What can I contribute here? What can I give?" People who choose to live life in that way inspire us and allow us to be in touch with our own natural inclination to give.

Then look around at the apathy, greed, violence, child abuse and discrimination in the world, and you know that there are takers as well. People who ask: "What's in it for me? What can I get?"

You and I have plenty of excuses for being takers. Ultimately those excuses all come back to our underlying beliefs. You might believe you have only a finite amount to give, as if you'll somehow show up empty, like a car that has run out of gas, when you give. People are actually the opposite of motor vehicles. We are only empty when we don't give of ourselves.

Or maybe you gave to someone many times, only to feel like it was always thrown back in your face. Or perhaps you felt your giving went unappreciated. If you've experienced your giving being rejected, or unacknowledged, you probably have a belief that giving is either painful or not worth the trouble. Better to look out for Number One, you think, otherwise nobody else will. It is useful to remember that giving is, in a way, both a selfish and selfless act. It is a win/win game. Both the giver and the receiver benefit. What we know for certain is that in the game called "taking," nobody wins.

My former wife, Dianna, and I experienced the privilege, the joy and the challenges of adopting two children with special needs—Levi and Emily. Both experienced truly horrific beginnings to their lives with somewhat predictable behavioral problems when they joined our family. Often someone would say, with the best of intentions, "you're so wonderful to have done this for these children." We learned to simply say, in most circumstances, "Thank you" and acknowledge that yes, we did contribute to their development into wonderful young people.

What was more real for us—and what we learned many people could not quite accept—would have been to share openly how much each of us gained from whatever contribution we made to Levi and Emily. These children of the heart and spirit, through their respective and unique life journeys, assisted Dianna and me in healing our own damaged inner child. As they struggled to become whole in spite of their rough beginnings, they taught us so much and our gratitude is total.

I want to be able to say this in way that penetrates deep into your being: Everything I've learned about this complicated existence called "being human" and amplified by the experience of working with Levi and Emily and with hundreds of thousands of people, tells me that *most or even all of the average person's neuroses and hang-ups disappear when they start giving and serving others.* It's that simple. If you're feeling "down" or ineffective or confused or all those conditions where you're being in a less-resourceful state...just find a way to give, to contribute to others. Doing that will transform your experience of life from ordinary to extraordinary more than any other single choice I know of.

The mysterious mathematics of committed relationships

When two people, in a marriage, for example, are predominantly in the relationship to take, that relationship will quickly become a disaster. More often, people think relationships are addition problems. That is, they believe relationships work on the formula: $1/2 + 1/2 = 1$. Each person brings part of the strengths to the partnership—and two halves make a whole. In reality, relationships follow the rules of multiplication, not addition. The mathematical rule for relationships is: $1 \times 1 = 1$. One whole person multiplied by one whole person equals one whole relationship.

If both or one of the parties enter the relationship feeling incomplete, with low self esteem, or looking to take from their partner in order to feel whole, then the multiplication becomes $1/2 \times 1/2 = 1/4$. As I'm sure you've experienced, being in this kind of a relationship is worse than being alone. Two empty and needy people make each other feel even more inadequate—beginning at the moment the honeymoon, what my former wife Dianna Lynn identifies as the "romance trance," is over.

Mentioning my "former wife" twice means it is probably a good time to issue a disclaimer: a lot of what I've learned about committed relationships is a result of personal failure. Until recently I've been spectacularly unsuccessful at creating long term, bonded and intimate primary relationships. A lot of reflection and a significant amount of therapy tells me that I've often entered into relationships to fill a hole in myself. When the "romance trance" wears off, and when the reality hits that this other person cannot complete me and make me whole, then my personal demons take over and the relationship is doomed.

Loving relationships are based upon commitment and giving. It is in giving all of yourself, the good news and the not-so-good, that strong relationships are created.

> IF EACH PERSON IS LOOKING FOR THE OTHER TO MAKE THEM HAPPY — INSTEAD OF GIVING TO THE RELATIONSHIP — THEN COUNT THEM AS HALF A PERSON. AND ½ × ½ = ... ¼

Although most of us operate sometimes as the giver, sometimes as the taker, all too often our taker side becomes dominant. Based on our experience of life, especially the times when we were hurt or let down, we often develop a belief that people will take advantage of us if we give too much of ourselves. For protection, we shut ourselves down, become victims and want others to give to us. We become takers, not because of a cynical decision to deceive or misuse others, but out of a misunderstanding of how to create the loving, intimate relationships that we all want. We wait for the other person to give first, so that we know it's safe to be vulnerable, safe to open up and give. Of course, the other person is over there doing the same thing, waiting for us to go first, waiting until it's safe to give. And so, often, we end up as takers in relationship, in spite of our natural inclination to give.

Win/win looks something like this

Peter Sherwood, the producer and editor of this book, told me about an incident when he visited a newly opened school for the underprivileged in Macau, in China near Hong Kong. The Brito School was a ramshackle old building with yawning holes in the roof and only the most basic of equipment. And it was much better than nothing for the poor kids who went there. Peter told me that Mother Mary, the elderly nun who ran the school, took him on a guided tour. They stopped at a room where about thirty girls were learning to type, on high carriage typewriters that must have been forty or fifty years old. They were learning a skill that was totally useless out in the world. Peter was shocked. There and then he committed himself to finding computers for the school, though he had no idea where he was going to get them.

Returning to Hong Kong, he located the biggest office equipment distributor and called the managing director, Colin O'Brien, a man he'd never met. He told Colin what was needed at the school. The next day O'Brien called back, saying, "I told my wife what you need for the school. She said that if I don't donate some new computers, software, and a trainer to teach the staff over there how to use everything, she'll divorce me."

It was done. Three years later, Peter received a phone call from the same Colin O'Brien (whom he'd still never met). He said he's since left the company to set up on his own, and asked if Peter would be interested in handling some promotional work him. When they met, Peter was so impressed with the new venture that he got on the phone to friends and raised some badly needed capital for the company. He also bought some shares himself. That was in 1990. The company has since grown twenty fold, and Peter's shares have become quite valuable.

I use Peter's story because it is a great example of how operating from giving brings win/win solutions in ways that are unforeseen and often seem miraculous:

- The children at the school won through obtaining state-of-the-art educational tools.
- The teachers won by being able to contribute more and learn more themselves.
- Macau society won by helping to create productive citizens, not wards of the state.
- The company that gave the computers won, with some excellent publicity.
- Colin O'Brien and his wife won, experiencing the deep satisfaction of contributing to a worthwhile cause.
- Peter was fulfilled by his role in facilitating the project and felt good for arranging it.
- O'Brien's new company won, attracting support and capital to enable it to develop much more rapidly than originally planned.
- Colin O'Brien, Peter Sherwood and others made money in the new venture.

I returned to the USA after my first 12 years in Japan and worked to bring the ideas of awareness, responsibility and communication to corporations who wanted better business results. One of our facilitators, Howard Edson, had a public service commitment to John Denver's Windstar Foundation, a non-profit organization educating people about creating a sustainable environment. He told me that Windstar had organizational and people problems that our programs could really help. I met with John Denver and Windstar's Board of Directors, and agreed to donate our VisionQuest executive seminar for the Board and staff. Master Seminar Leaders Dennis Becker and Aki Takarabe joined me to conduct the seminar—a truly wonderful experience for all and the source of tremendous growth for Windstar—in numbers and in impact.

I then was asked by John and agreed to serve on the Board for three years and, personally and through my company, donated a substantial amount of money to support Windstar's work.

Some outcomes for me from these contributions:

- developing a great friendship with one of my heroes (and now being reminded to open my heart through missing John's presence in my life)
- learning so much about creating a sustainable environment and becoming clear about the world I want to leave to my children
- being introduced into John's many relationships, many of whom have since become dear friends

The list goes on and on. It's not a mystery. It's simple: Giving selflessly works to help you create an extraordinary life.

Ordinary People...

...believe in limits to loving

...convert early life failures into an attitude of "taking" and the behaviors of a "taker"

Extraordinary People...

...look for every opportunity to give to others—time, money, energy and support

...know that service is the rent we pay for the opportunity to live our lives on earth

~ 35 ~

WHAT IF?

*If tomorrow never comes
Will she know how much I loved her
Did I try in every way, to show her every day
that she's my only one.*

"If Tomorrow Never Comes"
Performed by Garth Brooks
Written by Kent Blazy and Garth Brooks

This book is dedicated to the memory of my friend, colleague and partner in creating one world, one people, the late Art Marshall. Art loved Garth Brooks and introduced his music to me years ago, so that would be enough of a reason to include part of a "Garth song." More importantly, Art lived his life and did his work in a way that inspired me and so many others. His very premature and tragic death reminds me and all who knew him of what is really important in our lives.

Look around you. The trees, flowers, birds, every animal and insect; every living thing. It's miraculous. And it is all going to die. You will too, and so will all of those you love. The time will come when you will have to say good-bye to people. You don't know when. It could be tomorrow or next week. Yet, we live as if it will never happen. We get angry with our children or our partner, then leave for the day or longer, forgetting that if something terrible were to befall them, our last words would have been words of resentment and frustration, not love. And we would have to find a way to live with that.

It is often said that no one on their death bed ever wished he'd spent more time at the office. No doubt, there are plenty of people who wish they'd spent less. I spent most of the last week of Art Marshall's life with him and was struck by how many times we exchanged direct, heartfelt expressions of "I love you."

We live in a fast-paced, high-tech world that seems to many to be on the edge of craziness. It's a world where information is zipping around the planet at the speed of light, and you and I feel obliged to keep up with it. And as if that is not enough, the pager and the mobile phone make it more and more difficult to have enough time for those who really matter to us. It seems as though we have to schedule appointments with our kids, as though they were business associates. This attitude is often combined with the flawed idea of spending "quality time" with them. In reality there is no such thing as "quality time." There is only time, and most of us waste a great deal of it on things that add little value to our lives and the lives of those we say we care about.

Technology is changing our lives—sometimes for the better and sometimes not. It cannot and will not change what is fundamental to the human condition. It will never change the way we are, or how we feel. The more technology we create, the more we seem confused, side-tracked with what we are conned into believing will improve our lives in the future. Always the future. Anything to get us off thinking about who we are right now, and how we might make our relationships more rewarding and loving. Too many times, all of that is put on hold.

Alone on your death bed, I seriously doubt that you' going to be saying, "Man, this future I've been waiting for is terrific…and that new Ferrari, the miniature computer, the cell phone implant in my brain, being able to travel from New York to Melbourne in 35 minutes…boy, that is really enriching my life."

Joe South said it well in the song, "The Games People Play":

> "Oh the games people play, now
> Every night and every day, now
> Never meaning what they say, now
> Never saying what they mean
>
> And so they while away the hours
> In their ivory towers
> 'Till they're covered up with flowers
> In the back of a black limousine."

What if tomorrow never comes? What will your self-evaluation be when you take that last ride in the black limousine? This might sound abrupt or harsh, yet perhaps these are questions you should answer now. How do you feel about the relationships with the people in your life? Is there some bitterness you should heal? Do you make a point of regularly telling your family you love them? Have you found a way to let go and forgive those who have wronged you? Have you forgiven yourself for whatever it is that has shamed you or made you feel guilty? In other words, are you too busy for the most important things in your life? Maybe, like most of us, you'll do what needs to be done, say what needs to be said…tomorrow.

In a November 1999 *Gentlemen's Quarterly* article about Frank Sinatra titled "The Loneliest Guy in the World," Sam Kashner quoted two of Sinatra's close associates: "In the last analysis," Brad Dexter explains, "Frank never understood his mentality. And if you don't accept your mentality, then you're incapable of ever enjoying any real happiness. Frank didn't. That's why he seemed incapable of moving on, of growing up." Peter Levinson, Sinatra's publicist, said "…to me, this great artist was a lost soul. And if you don't think Frank Sinatra was lost in the fabulous world he had made for himself, look at what it says right on his gravestone: THE BEST IS YET TO COME. What does that tell you?"

ORDINARY PEOPLE...

...don't know or forget or avoid what is really important in their lives

...get caught up in life's busyness and "forget to smell the roses."

EXTRAORDINARY PEOPLE...

...commit the time and energy to build loving relationships

...practice mindfulness, a regular noticing, an awareness of self in space and time

...know their priorities and live consistently with them

~ 36 ~

AND NOW (FINALLY):
HOW CAN YOU BECOME A NEW PERSON?

When the doors of perception are cleansed,
man will see things as they truly are, infinite.
William Blake

A few days after we entered the new millennium I watched, amazed, at a Japanese "lifestyle" report on television. It talked about a revolution taking place in Japanese society and the rapid erosion of traditional values. The example given was the thousands of Japanese teenagers with dyed blond hair and leg-breakingly high platform shoes. Sure, they looked pretty stupid, but what was really going on here had very little to do with breaking down thousand-year-old traditions, and a lot to do with a bunch of people miserable with who they are and how they look and prisoners of Japanese "groupism." I found it tragic to watch.

For these Japanese teenagers, the tragedy is not only that by the time they are in their twenties or thirties or forties, blond hair and platform shoes will look even sillier then than it does now, it's that most of them will experience a great deal of pain in accepting the reality that they are short and have black hair. They are not and never will be tall Californians or blonde Norwegians. Many will never accept it. They will go on to have their eyes rounded and noses changed to look more European (the rates for plastic surgery are higher in Japan than anywhere in the world—including Beverly Hills). That will not change anything either. They are and forever will be Japanese, with Japanese tradition, language, height, hair color and facial features…surgically altered or not.

Is this just some weird Oriental fad? Perhaps it is. And it is also a highly visible example of how most of us live our lives, unhappy with who we are and how we look, and hell bent on changing it.

So tell me...how?

Now that you've read this far, you might well be looking for some answers. How can you become a new person and live an extraordinary life? How do you rid yourself of those irritating traits and inadequacies that you hate so much? How can you make the necessary adjustments and be done with what you experience as imperfections and shortcomings?

I know how it feels. You're tired of your nagging blemishes; sick to death of the way you look, and the way your life is, especially when you compare yourself to many other people. The question is, what can you do about it?

Well, here's THE ANSWER you've been waiting for:

Forget it.

You won't change. And you can't. Not now. Not tomorrow, or at a minute past midnight on the 1st of January next year. Not ever.

There you have it. You are now, always were, and forever will be, the person you are. If you want to save yourself years of untold anguish, then here is something you can take with you to your grave:

People...don't...essentially...change.

You will never behave perfectly, or even close to your perception of perfect. And I can guarantee you this: You will absolutely continue to be stressed, exhausted, and feel like a failure if you continue to try to find the perfect job, the perfect body, the perfect partner, the perfect children and the perfect life. It will cost you dearly—in time, money, blood, sweat and tears. And whoever told you that being imperfect is wrong? And, anyway, what is perfect? Moreover, where did you get the notion that anything other than a perfect you is not good enough? You are already perfect just the way you are.

If you're like most of the students in our seminars, you're probably thinking, "What the hell is this all about? Why am I paying good money for this book only to be told at the end that I am going to stay exactly the same?"

After hearing this shocking news, your tendency will be to do what we spend our entire lives doing: fighting gravity, and devoting even more time and energy to being in resistance to what you've just heard. And being in resistance to who you are.

Resisting your shortcomings = pain

The whole idea of chasing perfection in our lives is based on the notion that there is a "right" way to be and to live. This is the notion most people base their lives on. We make a plan. We set a destination, a path to the "right" way, to close in on perfection. If you're like most of us, you'll see how this is true. The process, by necessity, demands that we resist and try to eliminate our shortcomings. Remember, what you resist will persist. You recreate your faults over and over again because that is where your focus is.

In resisting our shortcomings, our shortcomings persist. Our focus becomes what we see as our negatives. So, we stay exactly where we are, tired and frustrated. Resist your shortcomings, and your shortcomings will (unconsciously) dominate your life.

However, what if…what if we focused on our greatness instead of our shortcomings? What if you simply accepted yourself completely, surrendered to who you are, warts and all, and focused on your greatness? Following the formula for perfection and the "right" way to do things brings nothing but pain. Living this way inevitably eliminates real spontaneity, creativity and joy. When we focus on what's right and perfect, we miss the experience of the journey, and, as some wise soul said: "The journey is the destination." Life is all about the journey, the discovery process. You may reach your destination, but what have you really gained? Are you different now? What have you learned? The learning is in the experience—and so is the joy and fulfillment.

In our ludicrous efforts to "change" and to be perfect, we try to fashion a perfect world for ourselves. We start to imagine that we are actually in control of our world, which is further from reality than an all-parrot moon landing. The universe, our universe, is out of our control. We live on a speck drifting around in an infinite vacuum with countless trillions of other specks. Our world is in a perpetual state of perfect chaos and entropy, with everything falling apart and dying and being born haphazardly. Meanwhile, we try to make life as neat and clean and orderly as a computer research facility, when in fact it is more like a junkyard. It always has been, and it always will be, no matter how much fussing and sweating and striving we do to make it different.

Based on results, how's it working so far?

Do you see how crazy and wasteful and frustrating it is to resist the way you are? If you still think you are going to change, that the "plan" and your route to perfection will succeed, then ask yourself this: How many years have you been trying? And how's it working so far? Is the pain and the frustration of fighting your shortcomings and imperfections getting you anywhere? My guess is that you are finding it to be incredibly hard and thankless work. You are who you are. You were born that way. And you were born perfect, unique, and one-of-a-kind. Like the song says, "There will never be another you." Life is a series of choices. Here, you have only two:

1. Continue to resist who you are, and fight to eliminate your shortcomings.

2. Stop the resistance. Accept your uniqueness, focus on your greatness, and learn to love who you are. You are perfect. You are the source of all you experience. You are a gift to your family, your company, your neighborhood, your community, your nation… and to the world.

I can guarantee you this. If you take choice #2, it will feel like a truckload of exam papers has been lifted off your shoulders. You'll breathe a huge sigh of relief. You'll feel light and free, with the sudden awareness that you no longer have to try to be something you're not, or achieve the unachievable. You don't have to play games anymore, trying to impress people (they weren't impressed or fooled in the first place) or impress yourself. You can begin to live your life in self-fulfillment, instead of trying to meet the expectations of other people.

You can, in fact, choose to live an extraordinary life. My friend Peter Sherwood wrote the following especially for this book. It's a bit silly… and it's not.

UNIQUE BUT INADEQUATE YOU

If your nose is too big,
And your butt is too small,
Your skin's the wrong shade,
And celebs never call,
If you open your mouth
and say the "wrong" thing,
And your hair has the texture
Of very old string,

If your legs are too long,
And your arms are too short,
Or your eyes are too wide,
And you're lousy at sport,

Just think of the great thing:
There's no one like you,
And you'll never change that-
Whatever you do.

Living just for survival means
you lose who you are,
Survival for life is
much better by far.

The only perfection is:
You're one-of-a-kind,
And that's just right for you,
Now relax, and unwind.

You're unique and you're great,
Nothing left to arrange,
And the really good news is:
YOU AIN'T GONNA CHANGE!

Are you living to survive, or surviving to live?

You will never change. You are already perfect. When I heard that statement 30 years ago from the facilitator when I did the precursor of our current seminar, it was difficult to accept. "Being with" that thought for several months finally brought me to an actual experience that it was true—for me. I am already perfect! This was about the happiest day of my life. Suddenly, I realized that I didn't have to try to be perfect, or to be someone I was not. I was already a perfect one-of-a-kind Robert White. No comparisons were necessary or even useful. It was a wonderful, unburdening moment, and the beginning of a lifelong journey that included much more joy and discovery.

You will never essentially change. Still, you can begin to define yourself through the choices you make. You can shift or drop beliefs that no longer support your growth. You can move beyond your self-imposed limitations. You can live from responsibility instead of victimhood. You can choose to be more aware. You can dramatically improve your communication with those you wish to connect with and influence. You very definitely are able to change and expand the way you live your life. In short, you can change your results from ordinary to extraordinary.

You do have the possibility and the resources to enrich your life, to have it be more meaningful. You can enjoy a more fulfilling relationship with family, friends, colleagues at work and—most importantly of all—with yourself. You can have greater self-esteem, passion and live life with a renewed sense of direction, purpose, and confidence. In short, your experience of your life can be extraordinary.

All of these things are within your reach. Changing who you essentially are is not. For that you should be grateful. You now need to decide if you want to experience all of the above, by living responsibly, or none of the above, by being a victim. Choose responsibility, then almost anything is possible.

I am going to ask you a question I asked earlier in this book: Are you living to survive, or surviving to live? Most people are doing the former; giving up who they are in the name of survival. Of course it does not help. *Because you are not going to survive.* You are going to die. By living to survive you lose the only opportunity you will ever have to experience the incredible joy and fulfillment of YOUR LIFE as it really is, the experience of YOU as you really are, the experience of YOU living an extraordinary life.

I wish you every possible success in your journey to wholeness, accomplishment and peace, in your journey toward living an extraordinary life.

Let Us Hear From You

We'd love to hear from you with your tales of 'living an extraordinary life.' Whether your life was transformed from ordinary to extraordinary just in the process of living or you attended a seminar or even from reading this book, please share your story. We're planning a future book around those kinds of "turning point" stories and would love to include yours.

What was your life like before you 'woke up?' What happened when some fundamental shift happened that altered your life experience from ordinary to extraordinary? What's your life like today as a result of this experience?

E-mail your story to: robert@ExtraordinaryPeople.com or send it to:

Robert White
Extraordinary Resources
5200 South Ulster St. Suite 1109
Greenwood Village, CO 80111

Of course, should you choose to send us your story, we do reserve all publishing rights including the right to edit or excerpt.

Additional Copies

For a copy of Living an Extraordinary Life personally inscribed by Robert White, you may order online at www.ExtraordinaryPeople.com

Significant volume discounts for corporate or gift orders are also available.

Speaking Engagements

Robert White is an engaging, witty and wise speaker for corporate, government, association and community meetings. His programs on effective leadership, building powerful relationships and on "Living an Extraordinary Life" can be tailored to any audience. His appearances range from 45 minute keynote speeches to experiential half day workshops to high-impact, multi day explorations of his core messages about awareness, responsibility and communication presented in collaboration with our professional Seminar Leader team.

You may get information about Robert's availability and fees or further information about Robert's work with individuals or organizations by e-mail at info@ExtraordinaryPeople.com or by calling (303) 993-4640.

The Achieving Extraordinary Success Home Study Program

Eight hours of professionally produced audio plus a 53-page "Owner's Manual" originally published by Nightingale Conant. This updated and expanded version by Robert White with Dennis Becker won the 2011 Earphones Award from AudioFile Magazine as "Best Spoken Word Personal Development Program." Available in either CD or digital download formats at: www.ExtraordinaryPeople.com

Executive Coaching, Team Leadership Development and Organizational Culture Change Programs

Additional information about our high-impact experiential learning programs and coaching for individuals and organizations is available at:
www.ExtraordinaryPeople.com
or e-mail us at info@ExtraordinaryPeople.com

Reference Acknowledgements

In the process of living and then in writing this book, I was informed, inspired, entertained and enriched by the following books. I am grateful to each author:

Nathaniel Brandon, *The Six Pillars of Self Esteem* (New York, Bantam Books, 1994)

Hyler Bracey, Ph.D., *Building Trust* (Self Published, 2002)

Chin Ning Chu, *Thick Face Black Heart* (New York, Warner Books, 1994)

Paul Davies, *The Fifth Miracle* (New York, Simon and Schuster, 1999)

Annie Dillard, *The Writing Life* (New York, Harper and Row, 1989)

Wayne Dyer, *Pulling Your Own Strings* (New York, Funk and Wagnalls and Thomas Y. Crowell Company, 1978)

Victor Frankl, *Man's Search for Meaning* (New York, Washington Square Press, 1985)

Richard Gillett, *Change Your Mind, Change Your World* (New York, Simon and Schuster, 1992)

Daniel Goleman, *Emotional Intelligence* (New York, Bantam Books, 1995)

Gerald Jampolsky, *Love is Letting Go of Fear* (San Francisco, Celestial Arts, 1988)

M. Scott Peck, *The Road Less Traveled* (New York, Simon and Schuster, 1978)

John Polkinghorne, *One World, the Interaction of Science and Theology* (Princeton, New Jersey, Princeton University Press, 1986)

David Remnick, *King of the World: Muhammad Ali and the Rise of an American Hero* (New York, Random House, 1998)

Anne Wilson Schaef, *Meditations for Women Who Do Too Much* (New York, Harper and Row, 1990)

Alan W. Watts, *The Spirit of Zen* (London, John Murray, 1958)

Lin Yutang, *The Importance of Living* (New York, William Morrow and Company, 1996)

Ravi Zacharias, *Can Man Live Without God?* (Dallas, Word Publishing, 1994)

About the Author

Robert White is a frequent keynote speaker and workshop leader on organizational leadership, successfully handling rapid change, entrepreneurial success and being more personally effective.

Robert's experience encompasses over thirty years in the training industry. He was President of pioneer personal growth seminar company Mind Dynamics Inc., and was founder and President of Lifespring, Inc. He founded and served as Chairman of ARC International from 1978-2001 and worked closely with its corporate and individual clients throughout Asia, South America, Europe and North America. ARC International, under Robert's leadership, graduated over 500,000 participants from its high impact experiential seminars and served over 1000 corporations.

Robert White has "turned on" and inspired diverse groups including United Telephone, JPMorganChase, Young Presidents Organization (YPO), World Business Academy, The American Chamber of Commerce in Japan and Hong Kong plus Rotary Clubs from Aspen to Singapore.

Robert White has served as a vice president of the Instructional Systems Association, and has served as Asian regional vice chairman of the Pacific Basin Economic Council. As a member of the American Chamber of Commerce in Japan, he served as chairman of several committees, and as a member of the Board of Governors. Robert was elected a Fellow of The World Business Academy in 1999. The World Scout Foundation honored Robert as a Baden Powell Fellow; he is co-author of the award winning photo essay book, *One World, One People*; and author of *Living an Extraordinary Life*. Nightingale Conant released audio tape and CD home-study versions of Robert's book.

Living out his commitment to contribute toward a world that works for all people, Robert actively supports the Sarvodaya community development organization in Sri Lanka, The Kempe Center for Child Abuse and Neglect and The Adoption Exchange. He also serves on the Board of Directors of Plant-It 2020 and the Board of Advisors of New Dimensions Radio. Robert founded One World, One People Foundations in the USA, Japan and Hong Kong – non-profit organizations that have donated over one million U.S. dollars to charities doing environmental education and those working to end child abuse and neglect.

Helping others to develop extraordinary personal leadership abilities, capacity and effectiveness is Robert's personal mission. His other interests include current events, reading history and philosophy, being with his eight children and enjoying many styles of live music.

CPSIA information can be obtained at www.ICGtesting.com
Printed in the USA
LVOW021644210413

329350LV00001BB/1/P